The Life and Times of
Asher B. Durand

PREFACE.

THE various subjects that illustrate this volume have been selected not so much on account of their artistic merit as to show diversity of talent, and, again, because they were accessible and adapted to photographic processes of reproduction. Among those lent for this purpose, I am indebted to Mr. Robert Hoe for 'An Oak Tree;' miss Fanny Gilliss for 'Washington and Harvey Birch;' Mr. Frederick R. Sturges for the 'Portrait of Luman Reed;' and the New York Historical Society for 'The Wrath of Peter Stuyvesant,' belonging to the collection of the New York Gallery of Fine Arts. My acknowledgments are specially due to Mr. Alfred Jones for the gift of the portrait forming the frontispiece of the volume, engraved by him after a photograph. To those whose names are mentioned in the text as having furnished interesting material, I have to add my thanks to Mrs. J. Wordsworth Thompson for the use of valuable documents; also to Mr. Charles Henry Hart, Professor William M. Sloane, and Mr. Gaston Fay, for kindred services. Finally, my acknowledgments are particularly due to Mr. Philip Gilbert Hamerton for the benefit of his taste and experience in rendering this book far more attractive than it would have been without his sympathetic and generous co-operation.

MAPLEWOOD, N. J.,

August 21, 1894.

INTRODUCTION.

John Durand's *The Life and Times of A. B. Durand*

[handwritten marginal note: "30 yrs old at Chunk's birth, but only 4 intes colo in bot"]

A SHER B. DURAND (1796–1886) was one of the most important American artists of the nineteenth century, a central figure
as an artist, as a founder of art institutions, and as the acknowledged
leader of the American landscape school from his election as president
of the National Academy of Design in 1845 until his death at the age
of ninety. Durand's six-decade career spanned the period from the earliest efforts of artists and writers to construct a national cultural iden-
tity on through the mid-century triumph and, later, the eclipse of what
is now known as the Hudson River School. Durand participated from
the very beginning: first as a master banknote and reproductive
engraver; then as a portrait painter recording the features of Founding
Fathers as well as the mercantile elite of antebellum New York; and
finally as dean of American landscape painters.[1]

John Durand's biography of his father was published in 1894. By
then Asher was already a figure of the remote past, remembered more
as an engraver than a painter. The artist stopped painting landscapes
in the late 1870s. He spent the last decades of a very long life at the
family property in Maplewood, New Jersey, where he occasionally
received guests curious to interview a living ancestor figure in the history of American art. Durand's death in September 1886 and the estate
sale that followed in April 1887 briefly rekindled public interest.
Daniel Huntington (1816–1906), who had succeeded Durand as president of the National Academy of Design, commemorated his long-
time friend and fellow artist in a memorial address delivered at the
Century Association (of which Durand was a founder).[2]

When Huntington closed his remarks by observing that Durand's
"sons rose to manhood to do him honor," he was surely referring to
Durand's son John (1822–1908), also a Centurion and an art critic who
had long been a member of his father's circle.[3] John was in his early
thirties when he and William James Stillman (1828–1901) founded
The Crayon (1855–1861), the most important art periodical of its day.
John had petitioned his father to contribute the famous "Letters on

Landscape Painting" to the magazine in 1855.[4] The two may have drawn even closer after the death in 1857 of Asher's second wife, Mary Frank Durand. John, whose own mother, Lucy Baldwin Durand, had died in 1830, never married. After the Durand household relocated from New York to Maplewood in 1869, John seems to have served as the keeper of the flame, managing family affairs, providing information to visitors about his father's career, and endeavoring to secure the elder Durand's art-historical legacy.

John must have provided much of the information for Huntington's memorial address of 1887, having already begun to assemble the materials documenting his father's life and career well before the artist's death. John was driven by concern about the by-then almost complete eclipse of Durand's landscape reputation and was stimulated no doubt by his own work on a history of the Century Association published in 1882.[5] That same year, John sent family documents to the prominent historian Charles Henry Hart (1847–1918), petitioning him to expand these into a biography of his father. When Hart had not delivered a manuscript by 1891, John Durand took the task on himself, compiling a richly detailed account of his father's several remarkable careers as an engraver, as a portrait and figure painter, and as a landscape painter in *The Life and Times of A. B. Durand*, the illustrated volume that first appeared in 1894.[6]

Influenced by the socio-historical methods of French critic and historian Hippolyte A. Taine (to whom the book is dedicated), and having complete access to family records and documents, John reconstructed in some detail the local environment and family culture in which his father had been raised, as well as the milieu of antebellum New York.[7] He also provided his own vivid recollections (and opinions) about the New York art world. He assembled invaluable information about Asher's paintings and patrons, quoted liberally from Durand's correspondence and contemporary reviews, compiled a checklist of engravings, and included excerpts from the "Letters on Landscape Painting." The importance and value of John's contextual approach was acknowledged at the time of the book's publication. "With these sixty years of an active art existence," noted the *New York Times*, "Mr. John Durand has interwoven many incidents and episodes which in

their combination help us to the better understanding and appreciation of his much-revered father." The reviewer also recognized that
Durand's extraordinary lifespan conferred a unique significance on his
biography: "This handsomely illustrated volume ... is of exceeding
interest, for in the story of Asher Brown Durand, is to be found much
which has to do with the history of American art. The subject of this
biography, born in 1796 ... saw the progress of that native art which
he was too modest to believe he had himself helped to create."[8]
Naturally John's chronicle is celebratory of his father, as well as defen-
sive about the inferior status of "the American school of art" by the
1890s. Nevertheless the text yields a great deal of reasonably accurate
documentary and anecdotal information, so that the book affords
valuable mining for the more critical purposes of modern scholarship.
As important, *The Life and Times of A. B. Durand* still offers a highly
enjoyable reading experience for historian and non-specialist alike.

The important turn-of-the-century surveys of American art by
Samuel Isham (1905) and Charles H. Caffin (1907) drew heavily on
information from *The Life and Times of A. B. Durand*. John Durand,
by then a somewhat embittered octogenarian expatriate settled in
France, had the pleasure of seeing the success of his mission to reha-
bilitate his father's reputation realized. "I succeeded in getting
Isham's History of American Painting from London," John wrote to
Hart early in 1906, "and have read it with pleasure and profit. It is by
all odds the best history of the subject yet published. It is true what I
said that the treatment of my Father is a test of Isham's capacity to
write a history of American Art. Consequently, I have written Isham
a letter stating my satisfaction."[9] Indeed, we still continue to acknowledge the importance of John Durand's contribution in the fact that
every major publication on Asher B. Durand since then has mined the
rich contents of this captivating volume.

Linda S. Ferber
Vice President & Museum Director
The New–York Historical Society
June 2006

NOTES.

1. For the most recent study of Durand, including a historiography and bibliography, see Linda S. Ferber, ed., *Kindred Spirits: Asher B. Durand and the American Landscape* (London and New York: Brooklyn Museum in association with D Giles Limited, 2007), hereafter *Kindred Spirits* 2007. The major collection of Durand's paintings and works on paper (some 400 works) is at the New–York Historical Society.
2. Daniel Huntington, *Asher B. Durand: A Memorial Address* (New York: Century Association, 1887).
3. For John Durand see *Kindred Spirits* 2007, 21, 231-232.
4. The "Letters on Landscape Painting" are reprinted in full as an appendix in *Kindred Spirits* 2007, 231-252.
5. John Durand, *Prehistoric Notes of the Century Club* (New York: Century Association, 1882).
6. The Asher B. Durand and John Durand Papers are deposited at the New York Public Library with microfilm copies at the Archives of American Art, Smithsonian Institution, Washington, D.C. The correspondence between John Durand and Charles Henry Hart is cited in *Kindred Spirits* 2007, 25. Thanks are due to Sarah Barr Snook for her survey of the contents of the John Durand Papers.
7. John Durand was a translator of Hippolyte Taine's (1828–1893) works on history and art, working with the eminent French historian until the latter's death. John noted that his father, also fluent in French, enjoyed reading Taine in the original language.
8. "New Publications: An Early American Artist: *The Life and Times of A.B. Durand.* By John Durand. 12mo. New-York: Charles Scribner's Sons," *New York Times* (February 10, 1895):27.
9. John Durand Letters, John Durand to Charles Henry Hart, February 1, 1906, John Durand Papers, Manuscript and Archives Division, New York Public Library, Astor, Lenox and Tilden Foundations, Archives of American Art microfilm reel N22, frames 56-58.

CONTENTS.

LUMAN REED.
1833–1836.

THE PAINTING PERIOD.
1836–1869.

CONTENTS. ix

CHAP.   PAGE

X. Tour in Europe—Steamer Life—George Combe—'Old Masters' in London—C. R. Leslie—Sir David Wilkie—Appreciation of the English School of Art—A Masquerade—London and the Country—Switzerland—Italy—Works executed in Florence—Claude Lorraine—Life in Rome—Voyage Home—Icebergs—Arrival 143

XI. The Period of Production—Prosperity of the Country—The Art Union War—Benefit of the Institution—Record of Works—Resigns the Presidency of the National Academy of Design—Summer Excursions—Life in the Woods—Art in a Western City—Studies from Nature—The *Crayon*—Rise and Decline of the American School 167

OLD AGE.
1870–1886.

XII. Retires into the Country—Works produced there—Letter to a 'Patron'—Lays down the Brush for ever—A 'Surprise Party'—Evidences of the Esteem of Young Artists—The Interviewer—Closing Years—Characteristic Traits—Portraits of the Artist . 197

APPENDIX.—I. Extracts from 'Letters on Landscape Painting,' published in the *Crayon*, 1855—II. Reply of Horatio Greenough to a criticism by George William Curtis on the picture, 'God's Judgment upon Gog,' published in the *New York Tribune*, 1852—III. List of Engravings by A. B. Durand 211

LIST OF ILLUSTRATIONS.

LIFE AND TIMES OF A. B. DURAND.

CHAPTER I.

French Origin—Genealogy—Parentage—Colonial Times—Politics and Religion
—Amusements—Beverages, Food, Cooking, and 'Help'—Topography of
Jefferson Village—Influence of Environment on the Child.

ASHER BROWN DURAND, the subject of this work, is
of French origin. Jean Durand, his ancestor, a Huguenot
refugee from Toulouse, in the south of France, fled to
England and was naturalised in that country in July 1684. Jean
Durand emigrated to America, and there, now John Durand,
appears as a witness (February 8th, 1702) to a deed of purchase
from the Indians of the land on which the town of Milford in
Connecticut was built. In May 1705 he is a resident of the
town of Derby in that State, and applies to the Assembly for
'freemanship.' In May 1709, recorded as Dr. John Durand, he
is appointed a delegate of the town of Milford on an expedition
into Canada. His importance socially is attested by the following
official record : ' By vote, Dr. Durand shall sit in the second
seat of the square next the pulpit.' Dr. John Durand married
Elizabeth Bryan, daughter of a prominent merchant of the day,
and had eight children. The sixth of these children, named
Samuel, was born July 7th, 1713. Samuel Durand left Connecticut for New Jersey about 1740, and settled in the town of

B

Newark, where he married Mary Bruen and had six children. His second child, John, was born October 10th, 1745. On reaching manhood, John Durand established himself in a place six miles from Newark and two miles from Springfield, called, at a later period, Jefferson Village, where, in 1774, he purchased land and erected a dwelling-house.

How the progenitors of the Durand family conducted or occupied themselves previous to the settlement of the aforesaid John Durand at Jefferson Village is merely of personal interest. It is presumable that they attended to their own affairs and fulfilled their social and political duties like other folks, without claiming or having bestowed upon them any privilege or honour that could distinguish them from their neighbours. In colonial times, according to early records, the rank of a man in society was determined, as we have seen, by the location of his pew in the meeting-house, while 'no one was allowed to vote who did not belong to the Church.'* It is probable that they were thus qualified, but that, inheriting French temperaments, they lived like most genial people, content to take life as it comes and gratify their religious sentiments in their own way. Why they emigrated from Connecticut to New Jersey is open to conjecture. It may have been that they did so to enjoy more freedom of action, like many others domiciliated among the more rigid Puritans of New England ; or, again, and probably the true reason, they left Connecticut in accordance with the ' incessant movement to and fro of people seeking to better their condition.' In any event, it may be said of them that, as Huguenots, they were 'the fine flower of an accomplished people, men of active

* *Forty Years in America,* by T. L. Nichols, M.D. ; *The Emancipation of Massachusetts,* by Brooks Adams.

minds, austere morals, heroic courage, and often of refined manners.'* I lay stress only on the fact that the Durand family is of French origin. Certain qualities, talents, and works which distinguish a man are more readily appreciated when one knows from what nationality he has sprung, which is the case with the subject of this memoir.

John Durand, having provided himself with a house, married Rachel Post of Newark, a young widow with one child, whose maiden name was Meyer, November 9th, 1779, in the thirty-fourth year of his age. His wife was of Dutch origin. Judging by a portrait of her, painted by my father in her sixty-fourth year, she might be taken for a Hollander of the time of Rembrandt. This couple had eleven children, of whom ten lived to maturity. It is well to note, as a sign of the times, that all but two of these children received Biblical names; the two eldest only, Henry and Cyrus, being named in a worldly sense, while the others received names respectively after characters in the Old and New Testaments — Isaac, John, Elijah, Asher, and Jabez, along with Mary, Lydia, and Elizabeth. My father, Asher Brown, his middle name being that of a maternal relative, was the eighth in the order of birth.

It is necessary to convey some idea of the region of country into which my father was born, as well as of his social environment, both of which shaped his character and professional destiny. It is probable that the few houses, painted either dingy red or white, which stretched along the road at the base of the southern end of the Orange mountain, had no name previous to the Declaration of Independence, a document which rendered its author the most famous man of his time throughout the country.

* Edward Eggleston.

As a matter of fact, the few houses thus honoured could scarcely be called a village; there was no blacksmith's shop, no grocery and dry-goods store, no tavern furnishing a lodging-place for wayfarers, or a bar for toper or politician, and no church: its devout inhabitants, chiefly Presbyterian, generally walked, on Sundays, to the church of that denomination at Springfield, the settlement that gave its name to the township in which Jefferson Village was situated. The only public building in the village was a schoolhouse, a building which, as the centre of a hamlet, but symbolising a very different sentiment from that of its mediæval analogue, the feudal castle, in Europe, forms the nucleus institution of American primitive life. Distant from the turnpike or toll road running between the two large towns of Morristown and Newark, the former at this time with two hundred and fifty inhabitants, and the latter with one hundred and forty-one houses and a population of one thousand, Jefferson Village lacked the usual stimulants of trade and travel which beget 'business,' the source of all progress in America; and accordingly for a long time it remained 'slow' and deficient in local enterprise. To atone for this deficiency, however, Jefferson Village possessed picturesque and moral advantages. Situated in a valley, formed on the west by the Orange mountain, and to the east by the opposite ridge of high ground declining towards Newark and the sea-level, it afforded for the lover of nature the centre of a quiet, rural landscape, not everywhere to be met with. Generally of one story, each house was shaded by a pine, willow, or black walnut tree, while there was attached to it a garden for vegetables, and a door-yard containing a grass-plot and flowers; in front, close by the road, there usually stood a well-curb, with an 'old oaken bucket' suspended to a 'sweep,' by which any thirsty wayfarer, if he chose, could help himself to a drink. The house in which my father was born was built midway up the mountain; below it, on the opposite side of the road, came the barn, an apple orchard, cherry and other fruit trees, corn and wheat fields, meadow land, and a stretch of woods beyond; behind it were the sheds covering the oven and wash-house. The woods reached to the top of the mountain, where the eye ranged over a vast expanse of lowland, consisting of nearly unbroken forest; a spire on the horizon beyond a blue expanse of water indicated the site of New York City. A fair wind brought the boom of a cannon from the fort on Governor's Island, or a salute from a passing man-of-war, the only noises that reached the ear and reminded one of the great metropolis. A few steps back of the mountain to the west lay a wilderness, as it probably existed at the time of Hendrik Hudson, a primitive forest abounding with deer and other wild animals, and traversed by streams alive with trout. Game was plentiful — partridges, quail, woodcock, rabbits, squirrels of every species, raccoons, and foxes; while occasionally a hungry bear that had trespassed on the farmyards in the vicinity would be tracked to its den and shot. One of these incidents gave the name of 'Bear Lane' to a mountain road near the old homestead. The charm of wild solitude, the perfect repose of nature 'undisturbed by the voice of man,' which my father early enjoyed in his frequent rambles over this mountain, had much to do with shaping his taste for art. Such was the outward world in which he lived, and, it may be added, the school in which nature was his only teacher. We now turn to the human nature of Jefferson Village, likewise of a primitive sort.

American villages in colonial times resembled each other

in one particular—every man was obliged to get his living according to his aptitudes ; the chief end of man in all was to ensure the welfare of himself and family to the best of his ability and opportunity.   Nobody profited by inherited capital or superior rank ; if anybody possessed money enough to buy the land he cultivated—he was comparatively rich, and that was all ; but he had to labour like the rest, and derive his support, as well as added wealth, mainly from the crops he raised.   Mechanics, those who had learned a trade, carpenters, masons, and the like, bartered their labour for produce, while all sold both crops and labour at the best rates wherever they could find a market for them.   Mutual assistance in other respects depended on neighbourly goodwill and the general community of interests.   Everybody, in sum, derived his ideas of the common or public good from the cardinal principle of self-support, which principle, in the political development of the country, finally gave birth to the theory of self-government.

But it took time for the theory thus generated to make headway.   Political conceptions in those days emerged out of practical considerations ; nobody, except closet thinkers, undertook to solve social or political problems metaphysically. ' Citizens were inquisitive, seeking the causes of existing institutions in the laws of nature.   Yet they controlled their speculative turn by practical judgment. . . . They were adventurous, penetrating, and keen in the pursuit of gain. . . . Nearly every man was struggling to make his own way in the world and his own fortune, and yet, individually and as a body, they were public-spirited. . . . They *unconsciously* developed the theory of an independent representative community.'* Self-government—the delegation of personal rights to a representative, and considered as an abstract principle—really arose out of the slow and gradual comprehension by the people of the burdens of English taxation, coupled with the pretentions of the English Government to collect taxes by force. In Jefferson Village, before journalistic days, news of English encroachments of this sort spread in various ways. A neighbour would take a load of hay to market at Newark, and on his return home would tell what he had heard about the Stamp Act in his talks with others like himself, while standing by his waggon awaiting a customer. Another would encounter somebody who had walked over to Springfield and seen a passenger by the coach from New York, who had told him about resistance to duties on tea. Generally speaking, the most news was obtained on Sundays at the church door before meeting began, or, again, from the minister, who would communicate it privately, unless, when of great importance, he stated it from the pulpit. 'In the absence of newspapers and of travel, the Sabbath was the day for hearing and telling the news, and the meeting-house became a sort of central bazaar where local gossip could be interchanged. The church thus became a club, as the door of the meeting-house served as a bulletin-board. It was a club, too, from which exclusion placed an inhabitant of the town under a ban, and made of him a pariah.'† Whatever political discussion ensued always grew out of the effect of the news on common interests. On the promulgation of the Declaration

---

* Bancroft.

† *Three Episodes of Massachusetts History*, by Charles Francis Adams, page 751.

of Independence, the popular mind was thus well prepared to accept and act in accordance with its telling abstractions.

After local politics came religious questions. Here the metaphysical powers of the uncultivated human mind had full swing. The parson was now omnipotent. 'In 1735 Gilbert Tennent preached at Amboy (a New Jersey settlement only a few miles from Jefferson Village) on the comforting and encouraging topic of the " Necessity of Religious Violence to Durable Happiness." . . . . The spiritual shepherds were wont to feed their flocks with food abounding in strength rather than sweetness. . . . The religious atmosphere of the middle of the last century was dark with the heavy clouds of doctrine and theology. Foreordination, predestination, election, and eternal damnation went hand in hand with free agency. The effort to reconcile the conflicting dogmas provoked laboured sermons from the pulpit and prolonged arguments and discussions in the farmhouse, field, and shop.'* A few years later various civilising influences had modified this spirit; but there was still enough of it. Bigotry in Jefferson Village provoked the same moral virulence as in similar communities in New England. Intolerance, characteristic of the epoch in old England, prevailed as in the mother country.† The local intellect was a good deal stimulated by religious definitions and by criticisms of lax or refractory believers. A manuscript on foolscap paper, fifteen pages long, found among old family papers, in reply to some one who had questioned his orthodoxy, shows that one of my uncles had to prove thus elaborately that he was all right on the doctrine of

---

* See *The Story of an Old Farm*, by Andrew D. Mellick, page 213.

† See *A History of England in the Eighteenth Century*, by W. E. H. Lecky, vol. i.

Election. But theological rancour and disputes caused no disturbance in the Durand household, and because, probably, the heads of it gave them no countenance. My grandfather and grandmother, both of equable temper, were averse to any heated manifestation of feeling or opinion. The remarkably even disposition of their sons in after life, their ever kindly ways, the absence of guile in them, and a singularly honest, unworldly devotion to their respective occupations, were undoubtedly due to this parental trait.

Natural instincts and emotions cannot be kept down or suppressed by conventional religious or moral theories; it is, after all, through the free play of the former that civilisation makes the most headway. However humble a community may be, the members of it, men and women, old and young, will enjoy themselves in some way. It behoves us, accordingly, to glance at the sports and pastimes of people in Jefferson Village in these primitive days.

As to pleasure, if such a term can be applied to early American life, it was chiefly connected with work. The women held quilting parties, spent afternoons at each other's houses in the intervals between washing, baking, and ironing, and talked and gossiped over their needles. 'In addition,' says the author of *The Story of an Old Farm*, 'they made their own garments and many of those of the men; they spun their own yarn, wove the family linen and woollen goods, smoked and cured meats, dipped tallow candles, brewed beer, and made soap. Their pleasures were limited, being confined mostly to quilting frolics, apple-paring bees, and husking and killing frolics. The latter were when the men met at each other's houses to do the hog-killing when winter set in.' Young girls would assist in making rag carpets, and engage in spinning contests to see who could spin the most yarn in the shortest time.   Husbands and fathers, as at the present day, were so weary when the sun set as not to care much about recreation of any kind ; to them pleasure consisted of repose.   The young men hunted and fished, according to season and opportunity.   Riding behind a fast horse in a gig or waggon was one of their pastimes ; not to take anybody's dust, especially if accompanied by a sweet-heart, was their great pride.   It is needless to state that 'sparking' went on according to natural laws and sympathies ; camp-meetings, revivals, and even prayer-meetings were quite as often attended to see the girls and escort them home as for religious purposes.   Music, generally sacred, brought together the young people of both sexes for singing-school practice in the meeting-house.   In the winter, when sleighing was good, there were occasionally 'straw-rides,' in waggon-bodies set on runners, to some remote tavern.   'Perhaps it is a string of twenty sleighs, with as many couples, gliding through the frozen landscape by moonlight, with the silvery ringing of a thousand bells and shouts of merry laughter, ending with a supper and a dance, and then home again before the day breaks.'*

Beverages, food, and the cooking of it, are important national details, and must not be omitted in this sketch of American village life in colonial times.   Beverages may be classed as natural and unnatural in the sense of local or imported products. In Jefferson Village, where the well-known 'Harrison' and 'Canfield' apples grew, out of which the famous Newark cider was made, this was the principal *natural* beverage.   Add to this 'apple-jack,' distilled from cider and affording an excellent

* *Forty Years in America,* by T. L. Nichols, M.D.

alcoholic drink. Root-beer, a decoction of sassafras and other herbs mixed with molasses and water, formed another local mild drink, to which add elderberry wine and cherry brandy. The principal *unnatural* or imported beverage consisted of 'Kill-devil,' or New England rum, distilled from molasses, obtained in the West Indies by New England traders; this 'tipple of the poor throughout the colonies,'* formed one of the great exports of the so-called 'land of steady habits.' It was largely consumed everywhere, especially by farmers in summer when harvesting their crops. It may be added in this connexion that, in the national sin of intemperance out of which untold tragedies have arisen, the *rôle* of New England rum † as a moral ingredient in the psychology of American character is important.‡ Of other foreign drinks—except, of course, tea and coffee—wine, the beverage of the luxurious, was rarely found; few probably tasted it except at the communion-table.

* *The Story of an Old Farm*—applied, however, to Jamaica rum.

† 'From the molasses was distilled rum, which was in turn shipped to Africa and exchanged for slaves, the slaves being brought out in return voyages and sold in the South.'—*The French War and the Revolution*, W. M. Sloane, page 124.

‡ 'The cheapness of liquors prevented them from being measured in taking a glass. . . . Treating, drinking in company and in crowds, and this free dealing with cheap liquors, led great numbers of people into habits of drunkenness, many of them men of the highest ability and promise. There were drunken lawyers, drunken doctors, drunken members of Congress, drunken ministers, drunkards of all stages.'—*Forty Years in America*, by T. L. Nichols, M.D. As late as 1832 a friend and correspondent of my father writes from Pittsburg: 'With a single exception, I perceive nothing either in regard to the condition of the place or the character of the people which would render a residence here at all uncomfortable to me. The exception alluded to is the intemperate habits of a very considerable portion of the inhabitants, comprising persons of all ranks, grades, and conditions; but their manners in this respect are mending, and I am informed that already a great improvement is visible in the faces of those who have heretofore lived, moved, and had their being in Monongahela whiskey.'

Cooking and food must be considered together.   Cooking, in those days, was of the simplest kind, boiling, baking, stewing, and frying—the last the most universal, because it was the easiest and readiest mode of preparing a hot dish at short notice.   The good housewife of that day was as busy indoors as her husband was out of doors, and had no time, if she had the talent, to study gastronomic compounds or processes.   With a good stock of lard in the house, kept over from pig-killing time in the fall, she could, with very little preparation, fry a piece of ham, and soon complete a bill of fare for an unexpected guest with bread, pie, and cake, baked regularly each week, and of which, including preserved fruit, there was always an ample stock on hand. Next comes kind and quality of material for cooking.   Fresh beef was rarely attainable, mutton and veal oftener, and of course pig-flesh always in some form.   'Occasionally fresh meat was had, as it was the custom of farmers, when they slaughtered a "critter," to distribute joints and pieces among their neighbours for miles around, relying for pay on a return courtesy.'   The basis of alimentary supplies, however, in the way of animal food, consisted of pork.   If not in the house, this was always procurable in various forms at a neighbouring store.   When a hog, fattened at home during the summer, was killed in the fall, fresh spare-ribs lasted for many days, sausages for weeks, and salt pork eternally.   In winter, communication with the rest of the world was entirely cut off ; the rivers and streams were frozen, and the roads more or less blocked with snow.   It was accordingly necessary in the fall, before navigation closed, to lay in stocks of salt mackerel, dried codfish, smoked beef and ham, with one or two barrels of pork according to size of family.   Potatoes, carrots, and beans, with apples fresh or dried, and preserved cherries, constituted the principal supply of winter vegetables and fruits; these, with pumpkins and squash, were always available. Milk, eggs, and chickens, somewhat tough on account of an exclusively corn-meal diet, with buckwheat cakes, dough-nuts, crullers, apple sauce, pumpkin pies, and sweetmeats, constituted the luxuries and delicacies of the winter table. In sum, for five months of the year, the breakfast, dinner, and tea, for every family, everywhere, rich or poor, consisted chiefly of salt food and hot cakes, soaked with lard, butter, or gravy. When spring came, and with it a warm, balmy atmosphere that stirred the blood, it was both theory and practice to purge and purify it by regular doses of Epsom salts, boneset tea, or sulphur and molasses. This system of cooking, feeding, and purging, not confined to New Jersey, extended more or less over the entire country. Is it any wonder that people were carried off by bilious fevers or affected with scorbutic maladies, which then abounded, and that stomachs were impaired by drugs, pills, and indigestion — in short, that dyspepsia became, as it is rightfully called, the national disease!

One more housekeeping detail, which greatly added to its cares and toil, was the difficulty of procuring 'help.' It is needless to state that, after a hundred years of the country's development, and in spite of the modern improvements due to steam and electricity which have rendered domestic service less toilsome, this difficulty still exists. In those days, it was not easier to obtain a servant, a 'good girl' as is said, or 'the girls, as women servants call each other in American households,'* than at the present day. The household of a farmer who had a daughter fared pretty well until she was taken off by marriage

* *Democracy*, the well-known novel.

or death.   If he had no daughter, and could obtain one of a neighbour who had two, and she was willing to 'hire out,' as was commonly the case, he was fortunate.   This custom benefited the girl, for she was regarded by the family into which she entered as a friend on an equal footing; 'she assisted in doing the housework, associated on terms of perfect equality with her employer's family, and considered that she was conferring an obligation, as indeed she was.'*   She merely served an apprenticeship with persons who were interested in her, which apprenticeship fitted her all the better for subsequent duties on getting a husband.   Another peculiarity of village life must not be overlooked.   The dressmaker, travelling around from house to house, conveyed the news and gossip of the neighbourhood, and was always welcome; while the school teacher, billeted on this or that family, was ever a welcome guest.

It remains to give a final glimpse of Jefferson Village as it appeared topographically in its palmy days.   On the foregoing pages the reader may have obtained some idea of its primitive state; about 1815, after the conclusion of the war with England, Jefferson Village had grown or 'progressed' with the rest of the country.   It then numbered over thirty families, and was entitled to a post-office, which would have given it a certain national status.   Application was accordingly made to the Government for this important adjunct of social development.   In proof of the right of the people to make this application, my uncle engraved a map of the village, showing the sites of its various dwellings, 'institutions,' and streets.   On this map appear 'Great Maple Swamp,' 'Little Maple Swamp,' 'Turtle Lake,' 'Factory Pond,' 'Crooked Brook,' and the east and west

* *Forty Years in America*, by T. L. Nichols, M.D.

branches of the Rahway river, winding away to the south on the two sides of 'the Mountain.' There is a factory, a saw-mill, and two mines—supposed, according to tradition, to have been dug for copper, a meeting-house called 'Babel Chapel,' and a fortification, if a name goes for anything, called 'Bom Fort.' The names of the occupants of the dwellings are given, among which are 'Captain Smith,' 'Captain Sam,' 'Aunt Rachel,' and 'Neighbour Joseph;' also of the streets, which indicate a satiric vein, such as 'Dominie Lane'—where the preacher lived who held forth on Sundays in Babel Chapel and wove rag carpets at home on week-days, 'Grub Street,' 'Heathen Street,' and, lastly, 'Necessity Corner,' where the school-house was placed. Whether or not there was too much of a waggish humour in the delineation of this map—as, for example, the names of the streets, to which even tradition bears no witness, or whether the people did not vote as now according to the dictation of 'bosses,' or whether the postal department did not approve of trifling with serious matters—it is certain that its mines, its lake, its pond, its swamps, its 'institutions' and sawmill, all having disappeared like its old tenements and left scarcely a wrack behind, had no effect on the authorities. Jefferson Village is gone. Thanks to a land speculator of these days, who bestowed the name of Maplewood on a railway station built at his own expense near the village mainly for personal benefit, and which commemorates nothing but bygone maple swamps, Jefferson Village is scarcely more than an historical myth.

Such is the character of the primitive community in which my father was born. But he was not of it. None of its ways excited thought in his breast, or prompted and governed his action. Not being a rugged boy, as well as the youngest, and probably petted by his mother, he was not called upon to assist his brothers in working the farm, or to take any part in the village amusements and social gatherings. His aims centered on the mechanical pursuits of his father, as he watched these going on in a shop adjoining the dwelling. Out of doors, his pleasure-ground consisted of the 'illimitable bounds of nature,' where he roamed at will over the fields and in the woods, enjoying perfect freedom physically and mentally, and with no society but the creatures of his imagination. Extremely diffident, as he said of himself, in his boyhood, he would hide behind a tree or bush at the approach of a person or vehicle. Habits of this kind, together with the gentle ministrations of his mother, and the freedom from moral restrictions which beset a boy ever told that he has to make his own way in the world, furnish the key to my father's capacity and conduct in after life.

CHAPTER II.

Autobiographical Fragment—Character of Parents—School-days—The Grammar Machine—Apprenticed to an Engraver—Partnership with his Master—First Work—Engraves 'The Declaration of Independence' by Trumbull—Dissolution of Partnership—Trumbull and his Gallery.

THE foregoing pages afford a glimpse of the boyhood and environment of the future artist; we now turn to more precise statements, as recorded in the following autobiographical fragment, written at the suggestion of a valued friend, Mr. F. W. Edmonds, a banker and a fellow-artist of reputation in the American school of art.

'MY MUCH ESTEEMED FRIEND,

'In compliance with your request, frequently and earnestly urged, I at length commence the work of putting down some memoranda in the shape of an autobiography. Rousseau says in one of his letters, *Quoique j'aime à parler de moi, je n'aime pas à en parler avec tout le monde;* the plain English of which is, "Though I may like to speak of myself, I do not like to do so with everybody." This is emphatically my feeling; and from my knowledge of your frankness and straightforward character, I am satisfied that, of all my friends, you are the one most likely to appreciate my motives in this matter, and especially to exculpate me from aught that might suggest an unworthy display of egotism. My present purpose is merely to give you what may be termed a chapter of

D

incidents, and probably, after that, I may from time to time carry out to some extent their respective details.

'I was born on the 21st day of August, 1796, at a small village in the township of Springfield, county of Essex, state of New Jersey. My father was a watchmaker and silversmith by profession—at least, these were his principal occupations. He possessed, however, mechanical talent of great versatility, and could turn his hand as occasion required to such diverse trades that it would be difficult to say what he could not do, so far as the means were within his reach. When a young man, he followed the trade of a cooper for a time. An uncle on my mother's side stated in my hearing that he had seen my father actually manufacture from the rough nineteen barrels in one day. He often employed himself in this way within my recollection, making for family use whatever article was required of this description. In masonry, also, he was equally skilful; he would construct an oven, build a chimney, or plaster a wall equal to the best. I believe that there is still in the possession of some member of our family a brass gun which he manufactured entire, obliged as he was to make the tools himself. Besides being a universal mechanic, he was a farmer on a small scale : but for repairing clocks and watches he was unequalled in the country round about ; his fame in this respect was well established, and he was constantly pressed with business, disordered timekeepers being sent to him from distances of twenty and thirty miles by partial owners who were unwilling to entrust them to others of the same profession. A more industrious man never lived. Yet with all his industry and resources he was unable to amass anything beyond the means for a comfortable living, owing chiefly to extremely moderate charges for his labour and the maintenance of a large family of children.*

'My mother was in all respects a suitable helpmate. She was like him in industry and aptness; there was no requirement in household economy that she was not equal to; and for uniform, steady virtues as a wife, mother, and Christian, more than fifty years of unremitting toil, with many a painful trial, bear witness.

'But I will not detain you with details of my honoured parents further than to add that my father was a descendant of the Huguenots, driven by persecution to this country at the time of the revocation of the Edict of Nantes, and, as tradition says, a French surgeon.† My mother's maiden name was Meyer, of Dutch origin, direct from the early settlers of New Jersey.‡ I claim no ancestry at the venerable hands of John Bull. I am the sixth of seven brothers, and, if I may

* Furthermore, 'He acted as a moral counsellor to his neighbours. Temperate in opinion, cool in judgment, and inflexibly honest, they could confidently consult him in all their difficulties. Though a plain country farmer, he was not indifferent to literature, judging by his books, for he was a subscriber to *Gordon's History of the Establishment of the United States*, and he possessed the large folio *Brown's Bible*, an important publication of that day. His shop was a resort of prominent well-to-do men of the vicinity, where they discussed current political and social questions, serving as an intellectual exchange suiting the primitive habits of those colonial times. At the outbreak of the Revolution, our artist's father enlisted in the army, but the authorities, discovering his skill in mechanics, sent him back to make bayonets, the troops being sadly deficient in arms. In one of General Washington's reconnoitering rides on the mountain behind the Durand farm, his spy-glass was broken and was given to the farmer to mend.'—*Memorial Address*, by Daniel Huntington, President of the Century Club.

† At the time this was written my father did not know the genealogy of his family.

‡ My grandfather died in 1813, prematurely, owing to a severe strain in

judge by earliest recollections, the feebleness of my constitution was in proportion to the order of succession. I remember a keen sense of insignificance compared with the rest of my brothers. I was, indeed, a delicate child, and, in consequence of this, received a greater share of maternal solicitude, which circumstance has exercised an important influence on my feelings and conduct in all the vicissitudes of life.

'At seven years of age I was sent to the village public school, where I was instructed in reading, writing, and arithmetic, a little geography, and the whole of the Westminster Catechism.* This instruction continued for five or six years, often interrupted, however, by the expiration of the terms of the itinerant teachers by whom the school was

felling a tree on the mountain behind his house. My grandmother survived him nineteen years.

* Grammar must be added, although he does not mention it. The text-book used by him in this school, decorated on the cover with a pen-and-ink scroll of leaves surrounding his monogram and bearing this inscription, 'Bought July 8, 1811,' is in my possession. In mentioning his studies, it is probable that he purposely omitted this one because, as he often stated, he learned all the grammar he knew from a machine constructed by his brother Cyrus. This machine, the idea of which his brother got from an acquaintance, rendered the abstract rules of grammar and the definitions of the parts of speech intelligible by objective means, through a combination of mirrors, slides, wheels, and other mechanical paraphernalia, so manipulated as to show the reason why a pronoun should represent a noun, why the verb should express the idea of action, why the conjunction should indicate the link of connexion between words and phrases, and so on. For example, the reflection of an object in a mirror denoted that a word called a pronoun stood for the object or thing called a noun, the necessities of language demanding a term conveying the sense of that substitution. It is sufficient to state that this machine made clear the meaning of the abstruse words, indicative, subjunctive, potential, and infinitive, with the terms denoting the variations of the moods and tenses, by concrete images. It does not seem to have been adopted outside of the village or family circle of students. Its ruins still existed in my boyhood in the attic of the old homestead, afterwards burnt.

supplied. Intervals of several weeks often occurred, which afforded me a good deal of time to indulge certain tastes for outdoor diversions, as well as for sundry operations in my father's shop. The latter consisted chiefly of the manufacture of various metal and other trinkets, such as sleeve-buttons, arrow-heads, powder-horns, bows, and cross-guns, and, finally, the most absorbing one—engraving on copper plates—and which fixed my destiny.

' My father and two of my elder brothers were accustomed to engrave monograms and other devices on the various articles manufactured by them, and in this art I was early initiated. But I was not content with this, having shown some skill in drawing animals as well as the human figure, excited to do so by my admiration for the woodcuts in school books, and by the copper-plate engravings that fell in my way, especially by the tickets or cards of watchmakers placed in watch-cases, designed with one or two emblematical figures, and again by the simple vignettes on bank-notes. On examining these with a strong magnifier, I could not refrain from trying to imitate their, to me, wonderful mechanism. Never shall I forget the joy I experienced on finding, after a few trials, that my efforts were, in a degree, successful. In these attempts I was not only obliged to make my own tools, but I had also to invent them, there being no one at hand to instruct me. Gravers I could easily manufacture and use, but I discovered, in the course of examining prints, that there were lines and dots produced by some other means : through diligent study and research, I at length found that they were the result of a distinct process called etching. But I could not reach the secrets of this art so as to make it practically useful. I merely ascertained that the plate was covered with a peculiar varnish of wax, and that the lines were traced through this with a needle and corroded into the metal by aquafortis. I was told that it was white wax, and I made use of it, but, not succeeding, I abandoned the effort and confined myself to the graver. I have still in my possession one or two specimens of these juvenile productions, and even now I cannot look at them without a degree of surprise at the tolerable imitation of etching in rendering foliage and the ground, such appropriate objects in nature for the etching-needle.

'Among the many visitors to my father's shop, there were occasionally men of taste and intelligence, who, on seeing my efforts, agreed that he would do well to place me with some distinguished engraver without loss of time. One gentleman in particular, Mr. Enos Smith, who had lived in New York and was himself an amateur miniature-painter, took especial interest in the matter. He accordingly volunteered to recommend the said artist, and undertook the necessary negotiations and arrangements for my pupilage. At length my father consented reluctantly to part with me, in case terms could be made consistent with his means. After months of consideration by all concerned, my amateur friend proposed that I should call on Mr. W. S. Leney, then the most prominent engraver in the city of New York. The time was soon fixed for the journey. Accompanied by two of my brothers, I proceeded to Newark, where we were joined by my patron, as I may call him, and for whom I had conceived a strong attachment. Thence we proceeded to New York, walking to Elizabeth-town Point, and from there to the city by water in a periauger. We arrived in the evening, and put up at an old filthy hotel near the Battery, kept by a Jerseyman of our acquaintance. Never shall I forget the feeling of desolation which came over me on this my first visit to New York! I was then fifteen years old, and had never passed a day away from home—or, at least, from among my relatives. But still more vivid were the impressions of the following day, when, on walking up Broadway, I paused in astonishment at what were to me the splendid printshops in the vicinity of the City Hall! At no subsequent period in my life, even in the great picture-galleries of Europe, did I experience such profound admiration of works of art as was then inspired by this display of coloured engravings! I could have lingered and gazed at them for hours. But time was short, and we were obliged to hasten on to the upper end of the Bowery, where Mr. Leney lived. I remember continuing up Broadway to the vicinity of Grand Street, and then over hills and fields to St. Patrick's Cathedral in Prince Street, the walls of which were partially erected in the midst of vacant lots. On reaching the Bowery we were soon at Mr. Leney's house, and with what trepidation did I present my plates to him for examination! How gratified at his commendation, but how saddened and disappointed on hearing that he required one thousand dollars for the premium of admission to his *atelier*, and stipulated another condition, that the expenses of the term of my apprenticeship should be borne by myself!

'These conditions were so far beyond my father's means that all further negotiations were abandoned, and we returned home. But my zealous friend did not stop here: some months after this he applied to Mr. Peter Maverick, then the most prominent writing engraver in the country, who had removed from New York to the vicinity of Newark, N.J., within seven miles from my native place. Mr. Maverick consented to receive me, on condition that I would "find" myself and pay for my board at the expiration of my apprenticeship, at the rate of one hundred dollars per annum, agreeing to take me into his own family. These terms were practicable, and accordingly, just entering my seventeenth year, I took my seat in his engraving-room, regularly apprenticed to him for a term of five years. His residence was about a mile from Newark, near the Passaic river, a situation which suited my temperament, and so satisfactory was it that I may truly say that the first eighteen months of my apprenticeship were the happiest of my life.

'My career as engraver thus commenced in October 1812. My first essay was a copy in lead pencil of an engraved head three or four inches long, the lines of which I carefully imitated. The effort was satisfactory to Mr. Maverick, and he immediately set me to work on a copper-plate, a piece of lettering consisting of an old title-page to *The Pilgrim's Progress*. Mr. Maverick considered my execution of this task equivalent to one year's practice under the direction of a master, and from that moment gave me work to do on plates for his customers; the first one was a series of illustrations of Calmet's *Dictionary of the Bible*, a few of which contained portions of landscape. I remember with what delight I applied myself to etching and "touching up" these subjects. My progress was rapid. I soon surpassed my shopmates, and became the chief assistant of my master.'

This autobiographical sketch here terminates abruptly. It was never resumed, mainly for lack of time, and, again, because the writing of it was an irksome task. It is sufficient to state that the pupil soon surpassed his master, many of the works bearing Maverick's name having been chiefly, and some entirely, executed by the pupil. During this apprenticeship his principal employment consisted in making copies for New York publishers of English engravings, illustrative of editions of Shakespeare and other poets, vignette designs for bank-notes, which then began to circulate freely, encyclopædia plates, diplomas, and other miscellaneous productions. I find no example or record of original work done by him during his apprenticeship, which terminated in 1817, on becoming the partner of Maverick.

During the period of his partnership, which lasted about three years, the young engraver's reputation increased to such an extent as to render him principal in the firm, instead of subordinate, and therefore its mainstay. The business of the firm consisted almost entirely of that brought to it by his talent. Finally a dissolution of the firm took place, owing to the following circumstance, thus recounted in Mr. Huntington's *Memorial Address:*—

'His first original work in engraving, when, instead of copying the work of others, he engraved directly from painting, was the head of a beggar, known as " Old Pat," a painting by Waldo, and now belonging to the Boston Athenæum, and usually called " A Beggar with a Bone." Durand's engraving was so well executed as to call forth the admiration of Colonel Trumbull, who had, about that time, tried to engage James Heath of London to engrave his " Declaration of Independence," but who had declined to do so on account of the extravagant charge. He then applied to Durand, who was willing to undertake it for three thousand dollars, half the amount which Heath had demanded. Maverick wished to be joined in the commission, but Trumbull wisely demurred. Maverick objected, was offended, and the partnership was dissolved.

E

Durand was now his own master, and gladly received the commission. He was chiefly engaged on this large plate for three
years, and the result was the masterpiece we know so well.
In it he has preserved the likenesses with great fidelity, combining
a free and vigorous use of the lines with a broad and rich effect
of light and shade most attractive to the eye. It established his
reputation as a master of the art. . . . . Trumbull was greatly
pleased. In a letter to the Marquis de Lafayette, dated New
York, October 20th, 1823, he writes : " I have sent to you a
small case containing a proof impression of a print which has
been engraved here from my painting of the 'Declaration of
Independence' by a young engraver, born in this vicinity, and
now only twenty-six years old. This work is wholly American,
even to the paper and printing, a circumstance which renders
it popular here, and will make it a curiosity to you, who knew
America when she had neither painters nor engravers nor arts
of any kind, except those of *stern utility*." '

The publication of this engraving established the artistic
position of the engraver. Colonel Trumbull entrusted him with
the commission in 1820, and the engraving was finished, printed,
and published in 1823. The printing was done by an Englishman named Neale, imported for that purpose by Colonel
Trumbull, there being no one in the country qualified to do
that class of work. The plate was very large, and the giving
of so important a commission to an engraver so young was
hazardous, to say the least ; but so was everything connected
with the enterprise — especially the procuring of subscribers by
Colonel Trumbull himself among people who were not wealthy
and indifferent to art. My father reaped the most advantage
from it, for it ensured his prosperity. Always, when alluding

Goupilgravure

COLONEL JOHN TRUMBULL.

Reproduction of the Engraving made from the Portrait painted by Waldo and Jewett in the Trumbull Collection at New Haven.

to his early career, he spoke gratefully of the eminent painter who thus started him in life. Besides employing him to engrave the 'Declaration of Independence,' Colonel Trumbull painted his portrait, and their relations were intimate. I dwell on this circumstance because, in later years, on the establishment of the National Academy of Design by the body of artists which had then become sufficiently large to take charge of their professional interests, and who were dissatisfied with the regulations of the American Academy of the Fine Arts, of which Colonel Trumbull was the progenitor and President, he sided with his brethren.'* Colonel Trumbull died in New York, November

---

* 'In the local history of art, Colonel Trumbull's connexion with the American Academy of the Fine Arts, and the part he played in opposing the formation of the National Academy of Design, are of interest. Full particulars of the strife are given in Dunlap's *History of the Arts and Design,* and in the *Historic Annals of the National Academy of Design,* by T. S. Cummings. Both of these writers were his antagonists. Dunlap, in his *Life of Trumbull,* carries his spite too far. It would pass for malice were his statements not more amusing than convincing. In trying to convey the idea that Trumbull was ungrateful to his early friend, West, that he was more English than American at heart, and that in the treatment of his important battle-piece he was only commemorating the triumph of Great Britain, Dunlap overshot the mark. The truth is, that in his connexion with the American Academy of the Fine Arts, of which he was one of the organizers and the President, Trumbull was trying to make water run up-hill. The difficulty between him and the artists who seceded from that institution was not so much due to him as to a condition of things beyond his control. The plan of the American Academy comprised a permanent, as well as periodical exhibitions, lectures, schools, library, and other agencies in art education, copied from a foreign model—that of the long-established Royal Academy in England—and not adapted to this country, or manageable by directors taken from the non-professional classes. The public of that time cared very little about art; there were few artists, and the judgment of stockholders, whose authority in the institution grew out of the money they paid for their shares, did not fulfil the same ends as the more intelligent patronage of a king and a cultivated aristocracy. The mistake Colonel Trumbull made was in supposing that a kindred institution could be at once established in an entirely new

10th, 1843, aged eighty-seven years and five months, leaving a collection of his works at New Haven, containing, principally, his full-length portrait of Washington, to whom he was an aide-de-camp during the war, the small originals of the large paintings now in the Capitol at Washington, and a series of miniature heads of the eminent men and women of the Revolution, with a portrait of himself by Waldo, also that of his wife painted by himself—all of inestimable value in connexion with the commencement of the American school of art, to say nothing of their being priceless souvenirs of a distinguished patriot.   In anticipation of his death he had negotiated with the trustees of Yale College, New Haven, for a permanent resting-place for his works, together with a burial-place for his own and his wife's bodies ; the main conditions were an annuity for the rest of his life and a gallery for his works, with, underneath it, the place of interment.   These conditions were accepted ; the gallery was constructed and Colonel Trumbull himself arranged his collection to his own satisfaction.   At one end of the gallery hung his full-length portrait of Washington ; under this the portrait of himself by Waldo, placed there after his death, and that of his wife by his own hand, while in the ground under the floor reposed their bodies.   His directions in relation to his burial were, ' Place me at the feet of my great master.'   Long after the completion of this monument, containing so many inviolable records of the past, the Yale School

country.'—*John Trumbull*, by J. Durand, published in the *American Art Review*. In this connexion it may be added that on the dissolution of the American Academy of Fine Arts, its collection of works of art was offered for sale, with the privilege to the purchaser of selecting for 1500 dollars any picture he pleased. Among them was the fine full-length portrait of Benjamin West by Sir Thomas Lawrence, now in Hartford.

for the Fine Arts was established, and it was thought best to transfer the Trumbull collection, with the remains of the artist and his wife, to that building and place them under its foundations. Here they are, the paintings in an upper story, the annexe to a general exhibition of miscellaneous works, and the remains of the painter and his wife underground in the basement beneath. The reasons given for the transfer of these relics were, that 'the building which contained them was damp, the pictures were getting injured, it was difficult to take care of them, and the building was wanted for other purposes.' Those who remember the old gallery—a unique monument in honour of an illustrious patriot and artist—and consider the sanctity of contracts and of the grave, may question the soundness of the motives which prompted this transfer.

CHAPTER III.

Fourth of July Oration—Poetic Effusions—'Love and Moonshine'—Marriage —Michael Pekenino—Mental Training—Recreation—The 'Elysian Fields,' Hoboken—'The Battery,' New York.

THE foregoing details afford a general idea of the beginnings of my father's professional career. I now turn to other incidents which, to maintain a certain biographical unity, give a glimpse of his private life at this epoch, his mental traits, his reading, his associations, his recreation, his services to the public—in short, the experiences and fortunes of a personality of a certain time, place, and character. We must go back a little way. In 1817, two years after entering upon his apprenticeship, my father officiated in a capacity singularly at variance with any of his subsequent performances, that of a public orator. His 'fellow-citizens' of Springfield township selected him for 'orator of the day' on the celebration of the national holiday, July 4th, 1817, soon after the close of the war with England. The celebration was held at the Springfield Presbyterian Church. The usual patriotic procession took place, at the head of which marched the music, consisting of fife and drum, played by two of the orator's brothers. The character of the address, published by request in the Newark *Sentinel of Freedom*, may be judged by the following extracts. Whatever may be said of the rhetoric, the patriotic sentiment which inspired it suited the occasion and the minds of the audience :—

'Yon dazzling orb, as it towers above the horizon in all

the effulgence of resplendent day, smiles with unusual com-
placency on this eventful morning.

$$*\qquad*\qquad*\qquad*\qquad*$$

'When we contemplate the astonishing progress of this
Republic along the plane of continued elevation, when we
survey the splendid structure of our Federal Government,
the rapidity of our improvement in Agriculture, Literature,
and the Arts, together with the glorious achievements of our
immortal Heroes, and when in contact with which we see all
nature conspiring, subservient to advance us to the highest
pinnacles of glory—have we not cause to look up to Heaven
with eternal gratitude? Have we not reason to exclaim,
Happy America!

$$*\qquad*\qquad*\qquad*\qquad*$$

'America is the last hope of human greatness; and, warned
by the red Beacon blazing over the wide plains of tyrannic
desolation, let us shun the fatal path that leads to the waste
dominion. An eventful era is before us! The convulsions
of Europe portend some uncommon epoch, and the potent
hand of Revolution, now evidently lifting over Britain, may
raise from the ashes of a sinking monarchy the Phœnix of
a Republic. . . . In vain the tempest of ambition shall
thunder; in vain the indignant billows of convulsing anarchy
shall dash against its foundations; it [America] is the last
asylum for the rights of man; the hand of the Eternal guards
it from destruction!

$$*\qquad*\qquad*\qquad*\qquad*$$

'Soldiers in the cause of Freedom, I turn to you! [un-
doubtedly the Springfield militia]. To you we look for
redress when the inflated insolence of foreign powers trifles

with our long forbearance! . . . . Let not the fire of
patriotism dwindle in your bosoms! When you see your
liberty in danger, when you hear the groans of your murdered
brethren under all the agonies of the ruthless tomahawk and
scalping-knife, when you see your beloved wives and children
torn from your embrace and perishing before your eyes by
the ruffian hand of British cruelty, or inhumanly scourged on
their naked bodies for weeping at the sufferings of their
husbands—what are your sensations? I see the flush of
indignation crimson the manly cheek! I hear you exclaim,
Perish the wretch who would shrink from the field of battle
when such were his incentives to action!

*　　*　　*　　*　　*

'And you, fair daughters of America! . . . . In your
defence, the arm is nerved with sevenfold vengeance! To
your embrace, the war-worn soldier flies from the din of
battle, and all its hardships are forgotten—or remembered with
the highest gratification.'

The reader may probably exclaim, 'Enough!' It is
sufficient to add that this severe handling of the British was
listened to with wrapt attention, vociferously cheered, and
honoured especially by the plaudits of the fair sex, as verified
by a lady present on the occasion, who stated to the writer in
her old age, 'We were astonished that one so young could
know so much.'

But this address was not the only manifestation of his
patriotism. He had seen service in the late war of 1812,
which probably excited his ire against the British. His brother
and himself, so he told me in after days, had been called out

along with other conscripts, and served one day somewhere
back of Brooklyn, to assist in digging and throwing up
entrenchments against a supposed landing of the British enemy
on Long Island.

We have now to turn to inspiration of a more peaceable
stamp. A couple of letters found among my father's correspondence show that he was not only guilty of oratory, but
of poetry in the shape of odes, which, if published at all,
appeared anonymously. His correspondent, at all events, asked
for copies of them. One of these odes was addressed to South
Orange and the other to Springfield, the two large settlements
of the township in which he was born. A rhyming reply
to his friend's letter shows the working of the poetic vein,
so natural at the sentimental stage of life. He apologises
for not responding to the application sooner :—

> ' But all the excuse that I shall make
> (Which, as you please, refuse or take)
> Shall follow here—then, first and last,
> Since you to other scenes have passed,
> And crossed the Rubicon of Love—
> Oh! how could I so heedless prove
> As, from this Bachelorian shore,
> To send my wonted nonsense o'er !
> I thought 'twould prove intrusive there,
> And cloud thy blissful Heaven so fair ;
> Besides, I've lived so long alone,
> My heart has grown as cold as stone,
> So that the muse that once look'd on me
> Has watched her chance, and now she shuns me.'

F

Another effusion in the poetic line, although composed many years later for a special purpose, as its title shows, may here be inserted simply as a biographical item :—

LOVE AND MOONSHINE: FOR A LADY'S ALBUM.

Of all the themes that poets choose
On which to supplicate the muse
Most earnestly for aid—that is,
Of themes for pages such as this—
There's none so apropos, so clever,
As Love and Moonshine mixed together.
Moonshine and Love has been the theme
Of every poet's fondest dream
Down through all ages light and dark,
From Homer to McDonald Clarke.
But not alone the poet's eye
Rekindles as the moonlit sky
Awakes the glowing charms of Love—
Bright eyes below! bright stars above!
Warm on the artist's soul it flows,
And lo! the living canvas glows;
And every artist, far and near,
From Rembrandt down to Robert Weir,
Has with a moonbeam drawn a sigh,
As Michael Paff can testify.

And who that's past the morn of life,
With hope and expectation rife,

That has not sought the Paphian bower
    And wooed the Cyprian queen;
Or who, when Cynthia, queen of night,
Has shed abroad her silver light,
Hath never sought the pensive hour,
    To sigh unheard, unseen?
Let science range creation o'er,
Let stern philosophy explore
    The hidden depths of mind,
And let them spurn the wingèd boy,
They'll never find a purer joy
    Than woman's love refined;
And though they shun the moon's pale beams,
There's much of moonshine in their dreams,
    Of least substantial kind.

Judging by this correspondence between the young friends,
full of sentimental insinuations and allusions, it is evident that
my father was thinking of matrimony, if not already engaged;
in any event, his rhyming letter is dated April 27, 1820, and
the following year he was married and installed in a house in
Provost Street, now called Franklin Street, New York. The
date of his marriage with my mother, the daughter of Isaac
Baldwin, Bloomfield, New Jersey, is April 2, 1821. It is
probable that he was enabled to take this important step by
the commission to engrave the 'Declaration of Independence'
given to him by Colonel Trumbull.

One more correspondent of the same epoch who annoyed
and yet amused him, as well as all who had the privilege of
reading his letters, must be mentioned, an Italian named Michael

Pekenino; he was a stipple engraver, and had a table in the studio of my father, who harboured and helped him along mainly because he was a foreigner and unused to the ways of the country. 'Pekenino,' said my father, 'sharpened a graver in the most wonderful manner. He told me that if he could engrave like me, he would go to —— with the greatest plea-sure,' as he expressed it in his Dantean phraseology. Pekenino was often employed by New York publishers, and particularly by a Mr. Bartow, for whom he engraved the heads of certain English poets to illustrate editions of their works republished in this country at that time. How the Italian regarded his patron may be gathered from the following specimen of his English, taken from a letter dated May 22, 1822, at Phila-delphia, to which city he had then removed, as it appears, to escape prosecution for debt :—

'DEAR ASHER,—
        'Intreating Heaven, threatening Hell, cannot induce that adamantean Bartow to send me some money, and what is most infernal to my circumstance, I cannot get an answer from that obstinate being— in better terms, mortal stone! That publisher of poets did not, and do not, soften his heart at all in reading them! He is as much sensible as his mind is informed. I will write to him once more yet. I will, and it will be the last he shall receive not arrainged in good English.'

On another occasion he says :—

'This year the Supreme Agent is indeed employed in recruiting the best earthy souls, Mr. Bonani, my countryman, which has illustrated Philadelphia for some months with his drawings which art was master off—he was called to Washington, and there, on the eve to be married to a living specimen of de Medicis (oh, sadness to imagine!), the irre-vocable shears cut off the tread of his life.'

Pekenino wrote elegant script and boasted that the treaty of Campo Formio, or another of Napoleon's treaties, had been engrossed by him. He and my father engraved each other's portraits, Pekenino making his engraving after a portrait by Jewett, while my father made his after a portrait of Pekenino drawn by himself. At the close of Pekenino's sojourn in America, which chanced to be at the time Bolivar, the South American patriot, was a popular hero, he became impecunious to such an extent as to oblige him to raise money the best way he could; the plate of my father's head being in his possession, he erased the title of 'A. B. Durand,' and, adding an engraved framework around the head, substituted the title of 'Bolivar.' Many were sold, and occasionally impressions are now found. Pekenino, to finish with him, returned to Italy, the land of his beloved Dante and Petrarch, where, as he says in his letters, 'I can enjoy the society of my friends Morghen and Longhi.'

The foregoing experiences help to bring my father's mental training into clearer relief. It is evident that the common-school education of his native village was not of much avail in developing the powers of his mind; on the other hand, it was no impediment to intellectual activity. The habit of the boy in satisfying natural curiosity in his father's workshop, the privilege of roaming the fields and woods which kept his mind in fresh contact with nature, and the indulgence of feelings and sympathies indoors that required no theoretical training, was an education of the best kind. Then comes another advantage in his early ignorance—he had nothing to unlearn. If he lacked the education derived from books, methods of instruction, and school drill, he found a fitting substitute for

this in the knowledge gained by experience, and especially
by intercourse with others whose educational facilities had
surpassed his own ; intelligent, eager to learn, receptive and
a good listener, his mind absorbed all the intellectual nutriment that his purposes and associations demanded.

In 1821 his friend Sylvester Graham, of bran-bread fame,
an enthusiast of whom more will be said further on, had
my father elected an honorary member of a debating society
in Newark.   At these societies, often organized by young
men in towns and villages, the graduates of colleges and
others, for self-improvement, the insolvable problems of moral
and social destiny were generally discussed.   Much of the
subjective, metaphysical nonsense of youth here found vent.
My father attended some of the meetings, and probably
acquired ideas of general use in conversation.   His reading
at this time consisted mainly of the English poets, of whom
Goldsmith and Thomson were his favourites.   Their works,
presenting human life and character in harmony with his
rustic experiences, suited his temperament.   Goldsmith's rural
scenes and personages, the dramatic truthfulness and genial
humour of the *Vicar of Wakefield,* and especially of *The
Deserted Village,* together with the descriptions of the seasons
by Thomson, vividly presenting the life of the woods and the
charm of lonely haunts, answered to the longings of his
imagination.   In after years, many of the subjects of his
landscapes were prompted by these poetic souvenirs.   The
earliest fruit of this branch of the tree of knowledge is his
original design and engraving of ' Musidora,' his first effort
at idealisation, and of which more will be said further on.
How he occupied his leisure hours, of which he had very

MUSIDORA.

'With timid eye around
The banks surveying, stripp'd her beauteous limbs,
To taste the lucid coolness of the flood.'

Thomson's *Seasons.*

Reproduced from the Original Engraving.

few, there is no record, save my own recollection of what
he said about them from time to time during his life. His
evenings were almost wholly devoted to drawing. Models at
this period could not be had—scarcely a plaster cast of any
description ; engravings alone supplied him with forms and
figures to imitate or adopt as guides in composing original
works. Only three elaborate pencil drawings remain to show
what he accomplished during these years: the first two,
derived from inner consciousness, consisting of the figure of
' Musidora ' and another of 'Solitude,' and the last, a drawing
of his first child seated on the floor by his cradle. Other
recreations were few and far between. Family cares and a
limited income prevented much indulgence in this way. One
of his enjoyments was the theatre. He heard Malibran, and
attended the performances of the elder Kean, and of the
admirable group of actors of the old Park Theatre in its
palmy days, fully appreciating the superior dramatic genius
of that epoch.

His recreation thus ministers to his professional pursuits.
It forms an important element of his intellectual growth.
Possessed by the sentiment of art and a love of nature, he
wasted no time on society or in any sort of dissipation.
When spare hours occurred he betook himself to Hoboken,
where he supplemented the Orange-mountain rambles of his
boyhood by strolling under the noble trees of the Elysian
Fields, then a favourite resort of those whose experiences
were like his own. Halleck, Bryant, Verplanck, Sands, and
others, born and brought up in the country, engaged in
literary pursuits, writing for newspapers and the like, were
only too glad to ' steal an hour from study and care,' and

refresh mind and body in this charming retreat. The Elysian
Fields were then in all their glory. My father resorted there
on Sundays and the few holidays which gave him some freedom.
A horse ferry-boat still served to cross the ferry. On its
deck chance acquaintances would be encountered and join in
the stroll. On one occasion, an incongruous discussion on
Rousseau's social theories took place with a moody, discontented,
Radical printer, whom my father determined to avoid in the
future. At other times, a more congenial companion would
be encountered, and the problems of art would be discussed.
But poets, painters, and printers were not the only frequenters
of these grounds. It was a fashionable resort for ladies and
children. The fresh summer breeze on crossing the river,
followed by an unmolested frolic on the grass, were rare delights
to them. City aldermen, again—respectable at that epoch—local
bons vivants, staid merchants fond of good cheer, came at regular
intervals to a club-house on the grounds to eat turtle soup,
play whist, and talk politics. Unfortunately, on Sundays the
Elysian Fields became more and more invaded by ' roughs,' the
inevitable canker of public grounds contiguous to our great
cities, until at last this sort of population got to be so numerous
that good society abandoned the place entirely. Then came
' commercial progress,' with its disintegration of all things lovely,
its wharfs, piers, steamers, ' forests of masts,' and dirt. Broad
avenues had been created, existent trees fell under the axe, and
the Elysian Fields vanished from the face of the earth.* Mean-

* The Stevens property in Hoboken, of which the Elysian Fields formed a part,
was originally a farm belonging to a Mr. Bayard, an Englishman and a Tory, who,
on the outbreak of the Revolutionary war, went back to England and afterwards
became a general in the British army. Confiscated by the United States Govern-

while, the Battery in New York itself competed with its Hoboken rival for recreative supremacy, and secured the attendance of all who were not free to indulge in a country stroll. Its precincts constituted the fashionable quarter of the city. Instead of a five-o'clock tea, almost everybody took a five-o'clock walk on the Battery, except in winter. The 'lower ten,' who lived 'up-town' between the City Hàll and Canal Street, availed themselves of the privilege, and formed a continuous stream in Broadway every fine day, wending their way to and fro. Young men and young women — who, then as now, composed 'society'—were the most numerous, and flirted and gossiped to their hearts' content. Even sage business-men in dull times left their stores, not far off, and resorted occasionally to the Battery, to inhale some of its invigorating sea-breeze and bask in its genial sunshine. Fashion, however, finally moved farther up town, to Bleecker Street and Washington Square ; commerce and the demon of improvement asserted their rights, and the Battery, with Castle Garden, became a depôt for emigrants. It is sufficient to say of the Elysian

ment, the property was bought by Edwin Stevens, and is now in the possession of his descendants. Mr. Frank Stevens (through my friend Dr. A. M. Mayer, of the Stevens Institute of Technology) kindly furnishes the following information regarding the horse-boat: ' Boats have been propelled by the paddle-wheel, by horses or oxen for centuries. The Romans and Carthaginians both used them. Prince Rupert, the famous nephew of Charles I., made one. Savary patented one in 1698. But the application of the paddle in all these instances was to an ordinary galley or vessel. John Stevens, in 1812–13, built the first horse-boat arranged so that vehicles with their horses attached could drive directly on it. His horse-boats remained in use until superseded by his steam ferry-boat *Hoboken*, in the latter part of 1821 ; but one of the horse-boats was retained for emergencies until 1825. The plan was copied on the East River for the Catherine Street and other ferries, and was long retained on some of the other ferries on the score of economy. The last horse-boat was advertised for sale in 1837.'

G

Fields and the Battery, and to remark, in connexion with the life of old times, that in the transformation of these magnificent pleasure-grounds, New York lost two æsthetic landmarks never to be replaced.

Trusting that the reader will pardon this digression in behalf of old times, and which the plan of this work makes necessary, I return to the engraving period of my father's life.

CHAPTER IV.

The Profession of an Artist a hard one—Line Engraving a Fine Art—Nature of Art—Utility of the Artist in Society—Religious Sentiment: its First Inspiration—Gradual Growth of other Sentiments in Past Art—Fidelity of bygone Artists to Natural Perceptions.

MR. HUNTINGTON states in the *Memorial Address* that 'it is a mistake that engraving was at that time almost the only artistic pursuit in the country which could furnish a reasonable support.' I must be permitted to differ from him. Notwithstanding the evidence in support of this assertion, I find, on the contrary, that other artists than engravers had a 'hard time' in the pursuit of their profession. As late as 1828, Alvan Fisher, a landscape-painter living in Boston, thus writes to my father concerning his contributions to the New York exhibition :—

'You mention that two of my small paintings had been sold, but that the person had not paid over to you the money received for them. May I request you to obtain the money and forward it to me? Cash is somewhat scarce with me—as usual with the painters. Engravers, I believe, are generally in better condition in this respect than the painters.'

Twenty-four years later the situation is the same. An eminent landscapist, whose merit was recognised abroad as well as at home, thus writes to a benefactor :—

'You will, no doubt, think me very ungrateful in neglecting to write to you sooner, but my apparent neglect is the result only of

vexations and disappointments.   I have sold in the last eight or nine
months only four small pictures to my brother —— for 300 dollars ;
these I sold shortly after you left the city, and one hundred of that
went to pay a board bill contracted (in the country) last summer.   I
am, luckily for me, paying my board this winter for myself and family
(with the exception of my son) in pictures ; Messrs. S. and L. (keepers
of a hotel) kindly consented to do this, purely, I believe, to assist me.
. . . . . My son, poor fellow, is trying to get a situation on the Erie
Railroad.   His situation is my greatest trouble.   Hitherto, I have been
able to maintain him.   But now adversity so presses on me that I
have but little to spare, and it wrings my heart with anguish to witness
his utter inability to get his living by painting.   I have a wife and
two daughters to maintain, and God only knows what is to become
of them if I cannot sell my pictures.'

Three years pass, during which period the artist lives by
continuing to borrow money.   Apologising for not having paid
his debts, he says :—

'NORTH ORANGE, N. J., *January* 1, 1855.
'I sincerely trust that although I have been silent, you will not
attribute to me wilful neglect.   I need not tell you that the artist's
profession is a very precarious one ; it is impossible for him, do the
best he can, to procure more than is barely sufficient to maintain
himself and those dependent on him.   If you should see in my conduct anything that might imply a shadow of dishonesty, I beg, for
"Auld Lang Syne," that you will eject it from your mind at once.
You wish me to write you more fully about our new home.   Alas !
I do not feel as tho' I had a home yet, the times are so dreadfully
out of joint.   I am convinced, however, that, notwithstanding my
"penchant" for the country, circumstances will make it imperative to
remove to the city.   I am likely to be forgotten in this Town of
Hatters and end my days a melancholy man if I stay here. . . . . My
prospects for the present are gloomy enough indeed.   God help us!'

Nevertheless, as Mr. Huntington aptly says, 'The painters
supplied the engravers with material for their burin.   Trumbull

was busy with his battle-pieces, and often painted portraits. Vanderlyn had painted the portraits which enlisted Aaron Burr in his favour. Waldo was then a student, beginning to practise portraiture and eking out a scanty purse by painting signs for hatters, butchers, and tapsters. Some of those pictures of beaver hats, with their beautiful gloss, or ribs of beef and fat chickens, or foaming mugs of ale at the hands of jolly topers, which were swinging in the wind in our boyish days, were the handicraft of Waldo, as he himself told the writer. . . . . Jarvis, too, was starting on that series of the heroes of the war of 1812, some of which Durand afterwards engraved, and which now adorn the Governor's room in the City Hall.'

Line engraving, it must not be forgotten in these days of photographic processes, which have almost supplanted it and converted it into a ' lost art,' was at this period of art development, the sole means by which the inaccessible works of a painter, those of an ' old master,' or of any foreign or native artist, could be made widely known. Through the cunning of its technical process, a line engraving displays the principal elements of a painting—composition, drawing, form, gradations of light and shade, and the subtleties of effect—everything but colour. In competent hands the mechanical processes employed, like delicate sculpture, become a fine art, and the engraver a genuine artist. Sometimes his art equals, and occasionally surpasses, that of the painter whose work he copies. The ' Hemicycle ' of Delaroche, for example, engraved by Henriquel Dupont, may be classed along with the original in artistic powers of expression, while it has been said of the two works, Van Dyck's equestrian portrait of ' Moncada,' and

the engraving of it by Raphael Morghen, commonly called
'The White Horse,' that if either painting or engraving had
to disappear, it would be better, in the interests of art, to
lose the former. In 1822, engraving in America was the
only 'paying' art — that is to say, the only branch of art for
which there was a public demand. The public, however, cared
nothing for 'high art' in engraving, either in subject or
technical skill, like the Madonnas of the great Italian schools,
or the martyrs, saints, and allegories belonging to Renaissance
art. Patronage of American engraving depended on less lofty
aims. The American engraver had to employ his burin on
portraits of men or women of more or less local reputation,
or on familiar scenes that appealed to common sympathies, of
which very few attracted attention. My father's progress, of
course, depended on this order of taste. Public patronage,
however, was not wholly due to spontaneous instincts ; he
owed what he enjoyed of it more to the recommendation of
his work by native painters—Trumbull, Sully, Allston, and
others—than to public recognition of his talent. His aim,
consequently, was not to please the public, but to perfect
himself in his profession. Literally self-taught, he continued
to improve in the same way, by means and facilities which
his growing reputation afforded him. On establishing himself
in New York, he procured the best examples of the works
of eminent European engravers—Bervic, Raphael Morghen,
Wille, Sharp, Audouin, Strange, and the rest—and studied these
closely. All that now remains is to set forth the nature and
conditions of his progress. In order to make this clear, I
must claim the reader's indulgence for another digression.

To portray the nature and conditions of an artist's

career in a community like that in which my father was
born, and where he had to make his way self-educated and
self-supporting ; where the utility of art in the past could
not be estimated by accessible works in free galleries; where
men of artistic genius born on the soil, like Benjamin West,
were obliged to emigrate ; where architects, and especially
sculptors, like Houdon, were imported into the country to
model the form and features of its greatest man ; where
there was almost absolute ignorance of the artistic masterpieces of the world, the statues, the paintings, the palaces,
the cathedrals that have been held sacred by successive
generations of men—is not easy. Some explanation, therefore,
of the service of the artist to society is necessary to enforce
his value in a new community, side by side with other
recognised ministrants to social needs.

Generally speaking, Art is a distinct language, a language
of outward images, by which the character of human emotion
in the service of the ideal is conveyed from mind to mind
better than can be done with words ;* while the artist is
the psychologist who, possessing a keen insight into emotional
causes and effects, reproduces these in material or visible
form. Endowed with acute sensibilities and with that subtle
perspicacity which detects the spirit under the form, studying
shades and meaning of emotion in the countenances and
actions of humanity, observing the special traits which denote,
for example, vulgarity or nobleness of character — honest
brutes, as in the boors of Teniers, or commonplace beings
as portrayed by other masters of the Dutch school ; again,

---

* Horace says, 'That which is transmitted through the ear arouses thought
less vividly than that which is placed directly before the eye.'

sublime despondency as in the sculpture of Michael Angelo, rapt adoration as in the saints and angels of Fra Angelico, beauty and purity of feeling as in the Madonnas of Raphael —obtaining his subjects from history, from real life, or inventing figures which translate his perceptions — the artist 'holds the mirror up to nature,' and satisfies ideal longings objectively for which ordinary language is inadequate. His qualifications for this service are simply sensuous impressions combined with intellectual and emotional sagacity not found in men of other pursuits. Hence the function of the Artist.

We have now to see in what sense he is equally necessary with other labourers in society devoted to its common wants. The main condition of the artist's existence in a community is the public demand for his work. In this respect there is no difference between the artist and any other man who labours for the common weal. The man who paints, models a statue, composes music, sings an opera, or writes out his thought for a living, is, as far as his labour is concerned, on a par with the farmer who tills the ground, the mechanic who works at a trade, the merchant, the doctor, the lawyer, the engineer, or the navigator, all of whose talents respond to common social necessities. As with them, the greater the demand for the artist's labour, the more does he improve in skill and capacity. The only difference between their work and his is this: that while the farmer, mechanic, lawyer, physician, engineer, and navigator, labour chiefly in behalf of the material wants of a community, the artist labours in behalf of its ideal wants, for the cravings of the imagination due to emotions, sentiments, sympathies, and aspirations. That these cravings must be satisfied to an equal extent with real or material wants it is needless to emphasise, as human experience from the earliest ages gives it proof. The ever-recurring recognition and maintenance of the artist in society, therefore, is the sign of his utility. A few illustrations of this psychological and artistic development in the past will make this point more fully comprehensible.

Take, for example, the strongest emotion that stirs the human breast, the religious sentiment. At the dawn of civilisation, humanity strives to divinise the mysterious forces of life and nature, which are rudely recognised as favouring or thwarting human energies. In Egypt, for instance, divine power incarnated in every familiar living creature is symbolised by images of man himself, of animals, birds, reptiles, and insects, just as the Egyptian conceives their relative power and influence upon him for good or for ill, before and after death. Images of gods of divers shapes abound in this sense, from the smallest to the most gigantic, from the little scarabæus * to the colossi of Memnon, all of religious significance and in hierarchical order according to the kind of force which excites general awe and reverence. The more mysterious the force, the more colossal the symbol. The hieroglyphic language of Egypt is that of images. The Egyptian, indeed, seems incapable of entertaining an immaterial idea ; images of gods — symbols of all sorts of abstract conceptions in which the faintest analogies of organic life, human, animal, reptile, and insect are traceable—-surround him at all times, out of doors, in his home, at his meals,

---

* 'La perpétuité des transformations était à tout instant rappelée à l'esprit par le scarabée, l'hiéroglyphe du devenir, l'amulette par excellence, reproduit à million d'exemplaires.'—*Le Panthéon Egyptien,* by Pierret.

H

in the tomb, ever present as the visible substance of his faith.

The same instincts and motives animated the Greeks, but on a higher plane of civilisation. The Greeks, far more advanced in personal culture and in social experience, more refined in every way, more delicate and subtle in their perceptions, with greater sensibility and capacity for life's enjoyments, more moral and more in harmony with the world in which they lived, personified at first divine origins in the elements, and afterwards, not alone the functions of animals, as with the Egyptians, but human energies, intellect, and virtues, as these became revealed by superior social and political attrition. Chronos, Saturn, the Titans, and other deities, symbolised creative forces, and constituted the rude deities of primitive times;* in their wake, as Greek society progressed morally and intellectually, the Olympian deities—Zeus, Here, Ares, Hermes, Poseidon, Athéné, Aphrodite, Artemis, and the rest—bear witness to the keen insight of the Greeks into mental and ethical phenomena. Perhaps no more striking example of Greek genius in this respect can be furnished than the nice distinction of meaning by form in the statues of the wise Athéné, the voluptuous Aphrodite, and the chaste Artemis, all female divinities, symbolising so many special attributes of woman observed in the complexities of her life and nature.

The art of the Romans, as far as religious emotion is concerned, is substantially that of the Greeks ; their original art

* ' C'est au statuaire que revient le soin de conserver les types religieux. . . . L'humanisation de l'idéal s'est faite surtout par ses mains ; pendant plusieurs siècles, la sculpture a été un enseignement théologique.'—*Philosophie de l'Architecture en Grèce*, by E. Boutmy.

is represented chiefly by monuments like the Colosseum, theatres, and immense baths, revealing through architecture the nature of Roman habits and amusements.

On the advent of Christianity, the attributes of the Redeemer found artistic expression in allegorical symbolry, soon followed by His personification in mosaic. At length, as society became more refined, more humane, chiefly through the growth of respect for woman, accompanied by the protection afforded her by the Church, the Madonna appeared in art, symbolising another ideal attribute of the sex than the more material one which prevailed in antiquity. Next came artistic representations of the experiences, trials, sufferings, and exploits of the 'noble army of saints and martyrs,' which in fresco, on the walls of churches, in countless statues and bas-reliefs outside on church doors and pinnacles, impress on the popular mind ideas of new virtues, new traits of human character unknown in bygone ages. All these forms, figures, and architectural structures, due to religious sentiment and constituting the plastic language of a new faith, attest the utility of the artist in mediæval society.

The almost exclusive monopoly of art by the religious sentiment begins to give way in the Renaissance epoch. Other human emotions now stimulate artistic effort. Portraiture, indicative of admiration or reverence for eminent men and of beautiful or distinguished women, gains ground. Allegorical art, sculptural and pictorial on a large scale, embodies a multitude of subjects representing ideals of power, conquest, glory, and other civilising influences, in antique and modern designs —the vast gardens, fountains, palaces, and other insignia of monarchical grandeur that now render Rome, Florence, Venice, and Versailles famous through the works of Giotto, Raphael,

Paul Veronese, Bramante, Rubens, Le Brun, Le Notre, and a host of other capable artists. European art, again, becomes differentiated under the title of Schools, mostly national, the title originating in technical peculiarities, such as drawing or colour, and, again, of sentiment. The Dutch school of art, a type of this differentiation in contrast with that of Italy, becomes prominent, arising out of local, social, and domestic life, with all its commonplace surroundings. ' It exacts and provokes the representation of man as he is, and life as it is, both as the eye encounters them — citizens, peasants, cattle, shops, taverns, rooms, streets, and landscapes. . . . . Nature, in herself, whatever she may be, whether human, animal, vegetable, or inanimate, with all her irregularities, minutiæ, and omissions, is inherently right, and, when comprehended, people love and delight to contemplate her. The object of art is not to change nature, but to interpret her.' * As has been well said, ' Why should not these pictures, a special idea of life and society, one of the great historic ideas of humanity, be considered precious?' †

History thus verifies the utility of the artist in the practical sense in which the utility of other ministrants to social needs is understood. The artists of all time, in employing the forms of nature to express grand ideas, have ever been mindful of the faculties of the people for whom they laboured; natural objects have been depicted by them in accordance with visual laws common to everybody. Sensibility of the eye to outward objects with reference to form and colour, coupled with a ready comprehension of their artistic purpose, have at all times been understood

* *Art in the Netherlands*, by H. Taine.
† *Sydney Smith*, by André Chevrillon.

alike by both artist and observer ; the sole difference between them is greater or less delicacy of perception and greater or less refinement of feeling in detecting the significance of an object chosen to interpret an idea. Artists in the past have never entertained or had their minds swayed by subtle theories of colour and light like those now current. Never have the great masters sacrificed the spirit of a subject to mere technical display. Half-way art—the forced concord of pigments in semi-obscurity, literal imitation, and the grouping of objects without sentiment or beauty, the shirking of drawing, incomplete detail on account of decorative position—never absorbed their thought or guided their brush. Egyptian, Grecian, Mediæval, Renaissance, and Dutch art, the works of the past which still excite undying admiration, mean the same to us as to bygone generations, because we see nature the same as the artists who painted them. In recognising the integrity of past art, would we not do well to follow such examples, and keep art from degenerating into mere technical bravura?

CHAPTER V.

Dunlap offers a Commission—Various Portraits Engraved—Clergymen, Patriots, Actors, and Physicians—The 'Annual'—Foreign Reputation of American Artists—Exhibitions—Rise of Art Institutions—The Press—Letter of James Fennimore Cooper—Collection of Philip Hone—Michael Paff—Fashion in Art.

SOME time before Colonel Trumbull had engaged my father to engrave the 'Declaration of Independence,' Mr. Dunlap, author of the *History of the Progress of the Arts of Design in the United States*, had noticed his talent, and sent him the following letter:—

'MR. DURAND,   'NORFOLK, *December* 24, 1819.

SIR,—By an arrangement with Bishop Moore, I am to paint his portrait in Richmond. I am induced to believe that a very great subscription can be obtained for a print representing this popular gentleman in this State alone, and important additions in Pennsylvania, New Jersey, and New York. In this State I am assured of active agency for this purpose. Now, Sir, the object of this letter is to ask you if you will engage in the scheme of publishing such a portrait, and share with me in the proceeds. If you are willing, the next question is, on what terms? I will deliver the portrait to you in New York next spring. In the meantime I will procure subscribers in Virginia, and on my route homeward in Washington, Baltimore, Philadelphia, &c. The size which has been mentioned is that of " Bishop White." At what price ought such a portrait to be sold or delivered to subscribers? How many inches is that print? Your answers to these queries, and any other information on the subject, addressed to me in Norfolk will, in case I have gone to Richmond, follow me, and I shall be guided by the receipt of your letter.

'I remain, Sir, your obedient servant,

'W. DUNLAP.'

The proposal was never entertained, probably because the engraver would take no speculative risk in the matter.

As has been already stated, the 'Declaration of Independence,' representing a group of patriots well known to the people of the country, is the first production of my father's burin which ensured his professional reputation. This engraving was too large, however, to suit the popular purse. During the progress of the work, Colonel Trumbull personally solicited subscriptions; he was obliged also to mortgage the plate while in my father's hands, and never, probably, was fully remunerated by the sale of its impressions. Engravings of the same character followed immediately: 'Oliver Wolcott,' Governor of Connecticut, and, at a later period, a series of portraits of national celebrities. Meanwhile his graver was busy with the portraits of divines. 'Why do you not engrave the ministers?' said one of his friends to him; 'they'll sell like hot cakes.' Conspicuous amongst these in size, as well as in the reputation of the subject, were 'Rev. John M. Mason,' the 'theological thunderbolt of the times,' and 'Rev. John Summerfield,' distinguished for eloquence, and particularly for success at revivals in touching the conscience of his hearers. Next after these came the portraits of 'Rev. Dr. Milledoler,' President of Rutgers College, 'Rev. James Milnor,' 'Rev. Gardner Spring,' and 'Rev. Samuel H. Cox,' also 'Judge Elias Boudinot,' President of the Bible Society, belonging to the same category, all of New York; 'Rev. Eliphalet Nott,' President of Union College, Schenectady;' 'Rev. Dr. Sprague' of Albany; 'Rev. Dr. Dalcho' of South Carolina, well-known pastors enjoying local fame and still in repute as men of ability. 'This,' said Mr. Durand, 'was the most humiliating work I ever did. I used to get them up in conjunction with the painter,

The general public would not buy them, so we had to appeal to the ministers and the congregations; and hawking them about in this way, by personal appeals, I barely made a living by engraving them.'*

Following these came portraits of eminent patriots of the Revolution, statesmen and military heroes, most of which were engraved for the *National Portrait Gallery*, successfully published by James Herring of Philadelphia. We here find 'Washington,' twice engraved by my father after portraits painted respectively by Trumbull and Stuart; 'John Marshall,' first Chief Justice of the U.S. Supreme Court; 'Charles Carrol of Carrolton,' one of the signers of the Declaration of Independence; 'John Trumbull,' painter, aide-de-camp of General Washington, and diplomat (who gave my father sittings during the progress of the work); 'James Kent,' Chancellor and jurist; 'Gilbert Stuart,' the artist; 'Aaron Ogden,' Governor of New Jersey, after a portrait made by the engraver; 'Dewitt Clinton,' 'Alexander Hamilton,' and many others of similar consideration. For this class of works he was amply compensated. Two large engravings—'General Jackson,' full length, after a picture by Vanderlyn; 'John Quincy Adams,' after a portrait by Sully—a head of 'Crawford' and one of 'David Crockett,' are of special interest in this series of subjects. On the completion of the Erie Canal, the Common Council of New York celebrated the event and published a commemorative volume, for which my father engraved the portraits of two eminent New York citizens—'Philip Hone' and 'William Paulding,' the latter after his own drawing.

---

* From 'Asher Brown Durand,' an article by Barnet Phillips, published in the *New York Times*.

The next series of portraits produced by him in conformity with public taste consists of several popular actors and actresses, eminent in their profession, and engraved for a serial publication under the auspices of Mr. Francis C. Wemyss, of Philadelphia : — 'Cowell,' 'Hilson,' 'Mrs. Hilson,' 'Duff,' 'Barnes,' 'Mrs. Barnes,' 'Forrest,' and 'Macready ;' 'Hackett,' for George P. Morris, editor of the *New York Mirror;* and 'George Jones,' afterwards the Count Joannes, at his own expense. After these follow a group of physicians belonging to New York and Philadelphia : 'Thomas Cooper,' 'Philip S. Physick,' 'David Hosack,' 'S. L. M. Mitchell,' and 'Valentine Mott.' Other distinguished persons further illustrate the public taste for art : 'Noah Webster,' the lexicographer ; 'Lindley Murray,' the grammarian ; 'Robert C. Sands,' poet, publicist, and humorist ; 'Anna Braithewaite,' a religious enthusiast ; and 'Catherine M. Sedgwick,' author of *Hope Leslie.* Certain individuals, ambitious of immortality at the hands of engraving, employed my father at their own cost : 'Garrit Furman,' who wrote and published amateur poetry ; 'Rem Rapelje,' a 'worthy burgher' and author of personal memoirs full of amusing egotism ; and 'William Fuller,' a noted gymnast and professor of pugilism, delineated by C. C. Ingham at full length in the 'manly art of self-defence.' Classified by number and title, these heads consist of thirty-two portraits of clergymen, twenty-three portraits of patriots and statesmen, ten of actors, seven of physicians, and several of men and women unknown to fame, claiming public recognition in their own way. Embracing, as this classification does, a greater variety of notable characters than can be found in the works of any contemporary artist, we can form a tolerably

I

clear idea of the sentiments that inspired public taste for art
and encouraged the growth of art in the community.   In
sum, the public esteemed the portraits of men who ministered
to its religious and moral cravings, its patriotism, its amusements, its health, and its literary and other tastes, such as they
were.   In this respect the American community awards honours
through art much in the same sense as the Greeks, who first
immortalised their gods, goddesses, and heroes by statues, and
after these in a kindred spirit their statesmen, physicians,
gymnasts, and philosophers.

But a taste for art in the American community, as far as
this is exemplified by engraving, was not fostered alone by
that particular branch.   Publications arose which involved
the use of painting, in which the talent of native artists
found proper appreciation.   Foremost among these at this
period was the 'Annual,' a publication originating in England,
the object of which was to supply the public with a gift-book
for the Christmas and New Year holidays—a book of poetry,
prose, verse and tale, by known local writers, and illustrated
by native artists, the model of which is the 'Keepsake.'   Thus
far, in America, public taste for illustrations (as nowadays
exemplified by monthly magazines, of which the Annual is
the precursor) had been confined to editions of the English
poets, containing a few line and stipple engravings copied
from English originals, such as those executed by my father
during his apprenticeship, and afterwards by Pekenino; as yet,
no publication in general circulation afforded popular illustrations of ideas and sentiments growing out of the real drama
and romance of life, actual and historic, then stimulated to
such an extraordinary degree by the works of Walter Scott.

Native resources in literature and art accordingly came in play, the result of which was the American Annual. Our best writers of that day—Bryant, Halleck, Irving, Verplanck, Sands, and the rest—together with our best painters and engravers — Morse, Inman, Cole, Doughty, Weir, Ingham, Danforth, Cheney, Smillie, and others—contributed to it with enthusiasm. The most prominent annuals were the *Atlantic Souvenir;* the *Gift*, published at Philadelphia; the *Token*, published in Boston; and the *Talisman*, published in New York—all proving of great service in rendering art popular, and especially in the development of native talent. My father contributed largely, his graver being in constant demand for Annuals so long as he remained in the profession. His principal works in this line are as follows : ' The Greek Boy,' a portrait by R. W. Weir, of young Evangelides, then a student in Columbia College; ' The Sisters ' and ' The Wife,' after compositions by Morse; ' The Ghost of Darius ' and ' The Bride of Lammermoor,' after pictures by Inman; ' The Power of Love,' after an old painting, artist unknown; ' The Dull Lecture,' after a picture by Stuart Newton; ' The Gipsying Party,' ' Sancho Panza and the Duchess,' ' Anne Page, Slender, and Shallow,' after compositions by Leslie; ' The White Plume,' an ideal head by Ingham ; and a frontispiece to the *Atlantic Souvenir* after his own design. Most of these subjects, it must be noted, appeal to domestic sentiment, and all are within the scope of American imagination.

The correspondence of my father with Messrs. Cary & Lea, publishers of the *Atlantic Souvenir*, indicate the spirit in which the Annual was edited, as well as their appreciation of the talent and judgment of the engraver. In one of their letters, Mr. Cary

recommends him to correct the drawing of a certain figure—
which he often had to do in the works of other artists.   In
another, he is requested to examine the collection of Joseph
Bonaparte, Count Survilliers, at Bordentown, New Jersey, in
order to find desirable subjects to engrave.   Again, Mr. Cary
says, 'We have received from London a very fine portrait of
Tintoretto's mistress, of which you might make a beautiful
illustration for our book. . . . . I should like to see your graver
employed on a handsome female head, as I am sure that you
would make something to please the nation.'   Whatever this
portrait may have been, it is probable that it was not engraved
on account of its title, which would have been out of place and
objectionable in a book circulating so largely in the family circle.
In another letter Mr. Cary says, 'You mention a picture of
Inman's ; as we desire to make the work as American as we
can, keep your eye on it.'

Public taste for art, again, had developed unconsciously
through the experiences and fame of American artists outside
of their country, the same as its literary taste had improved
through foreign admiration of Irving and Cooper.   Allston,
Malbone, and Morse, contemporaries of these honoured writers,
had begun their careers in Charleston, South Carolina, where art,
at this time apparently better understood than in the North,
found a liberal patronage that enabled these artists to pursue
their studies and find appreciators in England.*   Vanderlyn,

---

* It is worth noting that Inman, in 1835, painted 'The Bride of Lammermoor' for Mr. Hugh Swinton Ball, of South Carolina. 'The Bloody Hand,' by
Washington Allston, was likewise possessed by an American of that State.
'Charleston is said, of all the American towns, to have approached (in 1774)
most nearly to the social refinement of a great European capital.'—Lecky, *History
of England in the Eighteenth Century*, vol. iii., page 289.

through the encouragement of Aaron Burr, accompanied them, and was able to study and obtain honours in France. The recognition of the works of these artists in Europe reflected honour on American talent. Allston, like West, would probably have become President of the Royal Academy had he remained in England. Morse, on his return, brought his knowledge to bear, and wrote and lectured on art.

Meanwhile, unable to live and study abroad, a few self-taught painters were groping their way at home with marked success in new directions. Doughty, Cole, Fisher, Hoyle, and others, inspired by the beauty of local scenery and its associations, painted landscapes of decided merit. Dunlap had exhibited about the country his 'Christ Rejected,' a very large canvas, poor as art, but well calculated, on account of its size and subject, to impress the popular mind. Ingham painted ideal heads, and likewise Weir, together with historical compositions. Inman produced figure subjects, establishing his capacity in the higher range of art ; while, at the close of this period, Mount, prompted by his love of humour, came on the stage and admirably treated the comic side of American rural life by portraying the droll characters he found on Long Island. Works by all these artists were engraved for the Annuals.

Other agencies quickened the public taste. Institutions for art arose side by side with those devoted to social needs, and first, 'The American Academy of Fine Arts' in New York, founded at the instigation of Trumbull, as already mentioned, projected in 1802 and chartered in 1808 ; next, 'The Pennsylvania Academy of the Fine Arts' at Philadelphia, chartered in 1805—both under the control of laymen. 'This latter institution,' says Dunlap, ' owes its origin to a few gentlemen in Philadelphia—seven lawyers, one carver, two physicians, one auctioneer, one wine merchant, and one painter.' More important than these, however, was the ' National Academy of Design,' and the most conspicuous, because managed by artists themselves, naturally the most competent to regulate their own interests ; this institution, moreover, furnished the public with periodical exhibitions, giving to it, as it were, an annual report of local progress in art, as well as a novel and favourite entertainment hitherto unknown.

Exhibitions, which are the most potent of all agencies in developing public taste, merit extended notice. Dunlap states that the first exhibition in the country, got up by a small group of artists in Philadelphia, ' was opened this year (1794) in that celebrated hall where the Declaration of Independence was determined upon and proclaimed. The pictures were borrowed from the citizens. This association of artists, of whose names I find only Charles Wilson Peale, Joseph Ceracchi, and William Rush, held their meetings at the house of Mr. Peale. Some other artists, and Ceracchi at their head, separated from the " Columbianum " (the title of their projected institution), and after the first exhibition it died. Ten years after Mr. Peale's first attempt, some of the most enlightened citizens of New York (1802), with a view to raising the character of their countrymen by increasing their knowledge and taste, associated for the purpose of introducing casts from the antique into the country. These worthy citizens, though none of them artists, called themselves " The American Academy of Fine Arts."' The casts were purchased by the American minister at Paris, Robert R. Livingston. ' When these casts,' says

Dunlap, 'arrived in New York, a building on the west side of Greenwich Street, which had been erected for a circus or riding-school, was hired, and the statuary opened for exhibition. This did not attract much attention, and, the funds of the society suffering, the casts were packed up and stored. After the charter was granted (1808), the use of the upper part of a building, once intended as a house for the President of the United States, but occupied as the Custom House, was loaned to the Academy, and the casts removed thither. They were again removed, packed up, and stored until 1816.' To continue chronologically: 'In 1805, Jos. Hopkinson, Esq.,' Dunlap further adds, ' stimulated by a view of the casts executed in Paris after the antique, which were in the possession of the New York Academy, and by his own taste and patriotism, proposed to several gentlemen of Philadelphia the establishment of a similar institution.' In 1810, says Dunlap, this was done under the name of 'The Society of Artists of the United States.' Early in 1811 'the first exhibition took place, and an address was made by Benj. H. Latrobe.' The 'Society of Artists,' a rival of the ' Pennsylvania Academy of the Fine Arts,' was finally dissolved, and the field left clear in Philadelphia to this latter institution.

Of the press in these days as a fostering agent of native art not much can be said. The *New York Mirror*, devoted to *belles-lettres*, furnished its subscribers occasionally with engraved portraits, and Dunlap, its art critic, reviewed the annual displays of the National Academy of Design in a dry, perfunctory manner. Whatever space in its columns was otherwise allowed to art, it was generally absorbed by the ' Old Masters.' Occasional correspondence, however, in the

daily journals shows the expanding taste for art.   The following
letter by J. Fennimore Cooper, cited by Dunlap, although long,
merits a place here, inasmuch as it shows the superior intelligence of its famous writer, as well as the beginning of American
development of sculpture in the advent of Horatio Greenough.
The letter is dated at Dresden, July 29, 1830.

'Most of our people who come to Italy employ the artists of the
country to make copies, under the impression that they will be both
cheaper and better than those done by Americans studying there.   My
own observation has led me to adopt a different course.   I am well
assured that few things are done for us by Europeans under the same
sense of responsibility as when they work for customers nearer home.
The very occupation of the copyist infers some want of that original
capacity, without which no man can impart to a work, however exact it
may be in its mechanical details, the charm of expression.   In the case of
Mr. Greenough, I was led even to try the experiment of an original.
The difference in value between an original and a copy is so greatly in
favour of the former, with anything like an approach to success, that I am
surprised more of our amateurs are not induced to command them.   The
little group I have sent home will always have an interest that can belong
to no other work of the same character.   It is the first effort of a young
artist, who bids fair to build for himself a name, and whose life will be
connected with the history of the art in that country which is so soon to
occupy such a place in the world.   It is more : it is probably the first
group ever completed by an American sculptor.

'The subject is taken from a picture in the Pitti Palace at Florence,
and which is well known as " La Madonna del Trono."   The picture is
said to be by Raphael, though some pretend to see the work of one of his
scholars in the principal figure.   The Virgin is seated on a throne, and
the principal subject is relieved, according to the fashion of the day, by
cherubim and angels, represented as singing or sounding the praise of the
Infant.   We selected two little cherubs, or rather two infant angels, who
are standing at the foot of the throne, singing from a scroll, to be transferred
to the marble.   They are as large as life, if one may use the term on such

an occasion, and are beautifully expressive of that infantine grace and innocence which painters love to embody in those imaginary beings.

' I left Florence for Naples before the work had been commenced in marble, and can only speak of it as I saw it in the plaster. In that state it was beautiful, and I can safely say that all the time I was in Italy I saw no modern work of the same character that gave me so much pleasure on account of the effect. It was universally admired, and really, I think, it deserved to be so.

' In the picture, these angels were accessories, and when they came to be principals, it was necessary to alter their attitudes. Then the painter could give but half the subject, whereas the sculptor was obliged to give all. Again, the former artist was able to produce his effect by the use of colours; while the latter, as you well know, is limited to lights and shades. Owing to these differences between the means and the effects of the two arts, Mr. Greenough had but little more aid from the original than he derived from the idea. Perhaps the authority of Raphael was necessary to render such a representation of the subject palatable in our day.

' I think you will be delighted with the expression of the youngest of these two imaginary beings. It is that of innocence itself, while it is an innocence superior to the feebleness of childhood. It represents rather the want of the inclination than of the ability to err, a poetical delineation of his subjects in which Raphael greatly excelled, and which, in this instance, has been certainly transferred to the marble with singular fidelity and talent.

' Agreeably to the conditions of our bargain, Mr. Greenough has the right to exhibit this little group for his own benefit. I hope that the peculiarity of its being the first work of the kind which has come from an American chisel, as well as the rare merit of the artist, will be found to interest the public at home. 'Yours truly,

' J. FENNIMORE COOPER.'

In the way of private collections of paintings, that of Philip Hone, of New York, in which native art was dominant, is the most remarkable. It contained 'The Greek Boy,' by R.

K

W. Weir ; 'The Delaware Water Gap,' by Doughty ; two small landscapes, 'Falls of the Kaaterskill,' and 'Still Lake,' in the Catskill Mountains ; two portraits, ' Lafayette ' and ' Kent,' by Moore ; a landscape by Hoyle ; portrait of ' Dewitt Clinton,' by Ingham ; with water-colour drawings by W. J. Bennett and Wall.   This collection also contained the fine picture by Leslie of 'Anne Page, Slender, and Shallow,' now unfortunately in England, and ' The Dull Lecture,' by Stuart Newton, now in the Lenox Gallery, New York.

Only one more agency, conspicuous in the modern development of art, remains to be noticed — the Picture Dealer, a natural product of the commercial spirit, and a proof that art at this epoch had got to be of some consequence.   This social ministrant to the public taste of the day is ' Michael Paff, Esq., an industrious and successful collector of paintings,' as he is called by Dunlap.   His specialty was, of course, the ' Old Masters.'   When any works of art of native origin were offered for sale, it may be said, in passing, they were generally found in the shops of frame-makers.   One of Paff's treasures, a small ' Last Supper by Michael Angelo,' which the writer remembers to have seen at auction under the superintendence of its owner, was claimed to be original by Paff, because, on the pavement of the room in which this scene is represented, a line of stones equal in number to the letters of the name, stood for *Buonarotti*.   It is needless to say that Paff proved the authenticity of other originals by similar evidence.   But as ' Michael Paff, Esq.,' will appear again in these pages, he is dropped for the present.

Last of all these agencies comes Fashion, the fickle goddess. Being an important factor in the art history of all times and

countries, she claims consideration. Two phenomena in all
lands attest the influence of Fashion on the development of
Art : one, an appreciation of foreign art at the expense of
native art ; and the other, diverse popular theories of art which
arrest or pervert the natural taste for it. In ancient Rome,
for example, Greek art and artists were ever in fashion. But
we need not go so far back—take Italy in the Renaissance
epoch, where the taste for art, outside of ecclesiastical authority,
was governed by the fashion for the antique. Early in the
eighteenth century, Claude Lorraine, Poussin, and Le Brun,
born in France, went to Italy (as afterwards West, Leslie, and
Trumbull, born on the American soil, went to England), to
study and practise art. The Italian school was fashionable in
France for nearly the whole of the eighteenth century, until
Diderot inspired the French public with the merits of local
artists, thus bringing the native school into favour. We know
the tyranny of the ' David' school under the Empire, born of a
Roman sentiment, and which impeded the growth of domestic
sentiment in art inaugurated by Greuze. In England, near the
close of the last century—where Richard Wilson, its great landscapist, lived, like Shakespeare, scarcely known to his generation,
except by his peers—the fashion for ' Old Masters ' prevailed until
Reynolds, Gainsborough, and Hogarth became glories of the
nation, and enabled the British school of art to be established in
the present century. What could infant America do—a colonial
dependence of England, using the same language, taught by its
thinkers, and imitating its customs—but remain artistically in the
orthodox fashion ?   ' Old Masters,' of course, became its accepted
standards ; its first lisps in art culture were in honour of their
works, or those supposed to be such ; the sanction of amateur-

ship consisted in the admiration or possession of some old canvas claimed to have come from the hands of Raphael, Michael Angelo, or Correggio. Such is fashion in art. Next in order come one-sided views and standards of excellence, based on theories more or less crude or ingenious growing out of technicalities, colouring, and drawing. Conspicuous among these are undue admiration of ' pre-Raphaelites,' on account of superior ' earnestness ; ' Impressionism, a reaction against excessive detail, equally as misguiding as the opposite extreme ; * decorative distinctions that serve as mere screens for carelessness, indisposition to study, and inadequate labour ; and personal ascetic preferences, all of which more or less mislead and pervert the public intellect. But as fashion in art will be further illustrated, I pass on to other signs and means of native art development.

* A distinguished explorer of Africa, M. Mizon, on his return to France, brought with him a young negress, twelve years of age, called Sanabon, who became for a time quite a favourite in society. One day she was taken to see pictures in the Goupil gallery, containing works depicting various subjects. On being asked what she saw, she readily and correctly replied trees, men, and animals, as these happened to be noticeable on the canvas. In an adjoining room were the works of an ' Impressionist.' Led to one of these placed on an easel and being asked the same question, she hesitated a long time ; she walked up to the picture and looked behind it, and finally urged to answer, she replied, ' It is a horse.' The intention of the artist was to represent the margin of a pool, where a woman was washing clothes, with a child standing alongside of her.

CHAPTER VI.

Engraving for Business Purposes—Hatters' Cards, Lottery Tickets, Diplomas, Ball Tickets, and Horses—Bank-note Engraving—Drawings of Vignettes— *The American Landscape*—Prospectus by Bryant—James Smillie—' Musidora ' and ' Ariadne.'

HOWEVER dignified or exalted a public individual may be, however refined the process by which art renders the character or beauty of a given subject, both are sure to be pressed into the service of business and pelf. For example, the first international exhibition held in New York displayed busts of Washington and Henry Clay in white soap, while, if I am not mistaken, the same exhibition contained a Scripture subject in bas-relief, including a figure of the Saviour, modelled in butter, and claiming position as a work of art. In the Paris International Exhibition of 1868, to which Americans contributed, the President of an establishment in our country devoted to bank-note engraving and printing, incensed at the non-admission of his manufacture among the fine-art productions of the world, threatened the direst consequences. My father's work had not been long before the public before his graver was called upon in analogous directions. Applications were soon made to him for business cards. ' As our American artist had to cater to commercial wants, so had Hogarth in his time. Here is a card of Theodore Clark, " Hat-maker, corner of Chatham and Pearl Streets," and one of " J. Wilson, superior beaver hat, 160

Broadway, N.Y.," with particular instructions, carefully printed, how to take care of a beaver hat in case it got wet in a rain-storm.'* Then followed lottery tickets, diplomas, ball tickets, and engravings of horses. A case of the latter kind resulted in full-length portraits of two famous racers, 'Eclipse' and 'Lady Lightfoot.' But the most striking as well as worthy employ-ment of his burin in this sense was bank-note engraving, already a prosperous business on account of the superior quality of its processes, by which counterfeiting is rendered at least difficult. The antecedent experience of the country with con-tinental money rendered a new style of engraved currency imperative, and henceforth a rapid development of bank-note engraving. Much of the engraver's time, consequently, during this period was devoted to this occupation. What qualified him for it was not alone mere technical skill, but his ability in composing and drawing suitable designs, called vignettes. Again, his elder brother, Cyrus Durand, possessing rare mechanical genius, had invented a geometrical lathe by which complicated linear designs for bank-notes were produced, so delicate and intricate that counterfeiting was supposed to be rendered nearly impossible. The two brothers, accordingly, were induced by a competent business man to form a co-partnership, under the title of A. B. & C. Durand & Co. (1824). The work of the firm soon surpassed that of similar establishments. All that is here necessary to state, in connexion with art, is that the vignettes executed by my father gave fresh impulse to the business. Their subjects, consisting of drawings of antique figures associated with well-known American personages, symbolising local institutions and pursuits, proved to be novel and 'taking,' as the reader

* *Asher Brown Durand*, by Barnet Phillips.

Goupil gravure

BANK-NOTE VIGNETTES.

Reproduced from the Original Drawings in the possession of J. Durand.

may comprehend by the following examples : Neptune drawn by prancing horses, with a ship under full sail in the background ; again, a stalwart mechanic, with a cogwheel at his feet, welcoming Neptune as he comes out of the water to greet him ; Archimedes on a cloud lifting the world with a lever, its fulcrum being a supposed American mountain peak, with a canal lock at its base ; a pretty female figure representing ' Justice,' a sword in one hand and a pair of scales in the other, with a bust of Washington behind her on a pedestal ; Franklin, seated on a chair, in relief against clouds streaked with lightning, and at his feet an open book in which we read ' Franklin's Works : Mind your business ; ' a graceful female figure holding a flagon and cup, quenching the thirst of the American eagle ; another holding a torch which illuminates the globe ; Hercules slaying the Hydra ; also the Laocöon, of doubtful business meaning, but all in honour of banks and every sort of occupation. More familiar with antique art than any of his co–designers, his vignettes exhibit a wide range of fancy, with a certain degree of grace and elegance in the figures which, appealing to natural instincts for beauty, made them attractive to the most practical minds. One of my father's correspondents had written to him that ' Bank officers want something serious on their notes ; ' while another adds, ' Bank presidents say that they have never seen anything like them.' The Chemical Bank of New York orders a plate with the portrait of Van Buren, then President of the United States, together with the figure of a chemist in a laboratory, both for the margin of a bank-note, with an eagle for the vignette ; in reporting this order to my father, who was out of town, his partner writes that the president of the bank desires 'to have the eagle present a ferocious, spirited aspect ; " I want you," he says, " to tell

Durand to give him the real steel-trap look." ' About ninety of
the originals of these vignettes have been preserved, and whoever
looks at them cannot but regret that delicate art of this description should have been bestowed on productions of so little
account. But they were remunerative, and may be considered
in the same light as the fine art of old times bestowed on the
decoration of armour, jewelry, and ecclesiastical utensils.

In 1832 my father's interest in bank-note engraving had
ceased. Rival companies had been organized which, rendering
competition more and more disagreeable, and involving extra
efforts on his part, worried him greatly. He feared the
absorption of his energies by work he considered monotonous,
to say nothing of the diversion from subjects for his graver
which he preferred, like the portraits executed by him for the
National Portrait Gallery. Moreover, in his leisure moments,
he was constantly painting, and gradually losing a taste for
engraving. It remains to notice only such works by him as
denote the indifference of the public for work of a more ideal
import.

As early as 1830 he engaged in an enterprise—based on a
supposed public interest in native scenery—called *The American
Landscape*, intended to be a serial publication of engravings
after pictures of well-known localities by native artists. Mr.
Bryant furnished the descriptive text. The prospectus composed by this eminent poet is here given. It reveals the origin
and purpose of the undertaking, as well as the illusion under
which its projectors laboured :—

'In a country like ours, rich in every class of natural scenery, it
is matter of surprise that no successful effort has been made to accomplish
a series of accurate views, so ample as to give an adequate idea of the

Goupil&gravure

BANK-NOTE VIGNETTES.

Reproduced from the Original Drawings in the possession of J. Durand.

aspect of our landscapes, and so well executed as to be worthy of a place in the portfolio of the discerning collector.

'There is scarcely any part of Great Britain, or even of all Europe, in the least distinguished for peculiar or striking scenery which has not been entered by the observing artist, the numerous productions of whose pencil, multiplied by the assistance of the graver, have been sought for at home and abroad. Nature is not less liberal of the characteristics of beauty and sublimity in the new world, than in the old. The perception of her charms is not less quick and vivid among our countrymen, nor will we believe that there is wanting either taste to appreciate the truth and effect with which her features are copied, or willingness to reward those who execute the task with success.

'On the contrary, the embellishments of our "Annuals" and the avidity with which they, as well as similar foreign publications have been sought, for the sake of the engravings they contain, are alone a sufficient proof that there is no want of competent talent among our artists, nor of taste in the community to ensure the most successful results to such an undertaking.

'These considerations have given confidence to the proprietors of the *American Landscape* to enter upon the present undertaking. They now present to the public the first number of a series of views intended to embrace some of the most prominent and interesting features of our varied scenery.'

Only one number was published, containing six engravings, all by my father : 'Weehawken,' after an aquarelle by Bennett; 'Falls of the Sawkill,' by the same artist ; 'Winnipisiogee Lake,' by Cole; 'Fort Putnam,' by R. W. Weir; 'Catskill Mountains,' and 'Delaware Water Gap,' after a picture painted by the engraver. The undertaking proved a failure, accompanied with loss. The engravings, it must be noted, are inferior in merit to others of the same hand, especially when compared with the admirable productions afterwards of Mr. James Smillie, who, then a young man, was employed by my father to etch the

'Fort Putnam.' In obtaining information on this point, his son, Mr. James B. Smillie, favours me with the following note, giving the only additional circumstances worth preserving in connexion with this abortive undertaking :—

'The little incident in the history of our fathers, of which you asked me to make a note, is briefly this : My father's family left Edinburgh, emigrating to Quebec. About 1830 he reached New York on a voyage of discovery, being then in his twenty-second year. He hoped to find in that city a wider field for his efforts as a landscape-engraver than Quebec offered. An utter stranger in the place, things went hard with him. After two or three petty and unimportant plates, engraved for the book-publishers, he met Mr. Robert W. Weir, then a young man just returned from his art studies in Italy. Mr. Weir was interested in the stranger and his work, and proposed that he should make an engraving after one of his paintings, the print to be published as a joint venture. (Think of the Arcadian simplicity, the sweet faith of those two youths !) As my father had no place where he could work, Mr. Weir offered him a window and a seat in his studio in Canal Street, and there he engraved the plate " Convent Gate, Palestrina, near Rome." Of course, as a commercial speculation, the publication was a complete failure. My father was discouraged, home-sick, and anxious to get back to his mother in Quebec. Winter was near, and such a journey at that season promised all the rigours and hardships of a journey to the North Pole. Your father saw proofs of the " Convent Gate," met my father and asked him to engrave some plates for an illustrated serial then projected. The offer seemed to present the desired opening to the new field sought by the young Scotchman. A kindly Scotch woman gave him shelter in an attic bedroom somewhere in Hudson Street, without fire, in the month of December, where he etched the plate " Fort Putnam, West Point." When the proof was presented to your father it was accepted with flattering compliments and new commissions were offered, but my father could no longer restrain his impatience to be away. The sum of forty dollars was paid for about four weeks' work, which was considered magnificent by the recipient. He bought for himself some needed garments and set off upon his mid-winter journey to Quebec, the whole distance being traversed in sleighs. This proved to be the opening. Another year and my father returned to New York, bringing his mother and younger brothers and sisters with him. From that time on the success of the young engraver was an assured and ever-growing one.’

The remaining works of the engraver, which attest both the talent of the artist and the indifference of the public to art beyond its comprehension, are those of ‘ Musidora ’ and ‘Ariadne,’ occasionally alluded to in the preceding pages. These works belong to the highest aims of artistic endeavour, both being the fruit of the artist’s admiration for the technical skill of the masters of engraving in the rendering of flesh. The former is an illustration of a fine passage in Thomson’s *Seasons :* Musidora, an ideal of female loveliness, relying upon the privacy of a sequestered nook in the woods, divested of clothing and about to bathe in a pool at her feet, stands in an attitude of listening suspense, as if arrested by the sound of an intruder. The design is wholly a product of ‘ inner conscious-ness.’ Lacking the technical resources of the draughtsman, his powers were inadequate for such a subject. Just starting in his career, with very little experience in drawing, coupled with the impossibility of finding a model for a nude figure at that time, the attempt was simply Quixotic. Naturally, the figure shows defects in proportion and what is called modelling. Neverthe-less, the landscape portion of the design is well executed, and likewise the composition and treatment of the subject — the attitude of the figure and its refined sentiment — two merits that render the work as a whole satisfactory. It is proper to state that, as far as remuneration for his labour is concerned, not enough was obtained by the sale of impressions to pay for paper and printing. Subsequently, the plate was borrowed by the printer, and destroyed in a conflagration of his premises.

'Ariadne,' the second attempt of the same order—from a masterpiece by Vanderlyn which came into my father's possession—was more successful from an artistic point of view. This engraving, the merits of which are sufficiently known, was finished about 1835. Notwithstanding that the original painting was always before him in his studio, he did not begin the work until he had made a reduced copy of it in colour of the size of the intended engraving, which he executed in a masterly manner, especially in accuracy of drawing and modelling, as well as in conveying the tone or effect of the original. But, as with the 'Musidora,' the 'Ariadne,' undertaken solely for the love of art, unconscious of pecuniary reward or public sympathy, was also, commercially speaking, a failure. The public proved scarcely more appreciative in the latter than in the former case. Amateurs of engravings alone obtained copies of it. Printing, an art by itself, was even then at a rudimentary stage. Skilled workmen could not be had. More than one-half of the impressions taken from the plate had to be destroyed on account of imperfections, while the greater part remained undisposed of even at the end of his career. The plate is now in the National Museum at the Smithsonian Institution in Washington.

To complete the foregoing details of the 'Ariadne,' the following is added concerning the picture itself. Vanderlyn painted the figure in Paris, where the requisite facilities for executing a work of this class were readily attainable; a charcoal drawing from life remains to attest these resources.

ARIADNE.

Reproduced from the Engraving of the Picture painted by John Vanderlyn,
in the possession of the Pennsylvania Academy of the Fine Arts.

Of course, an engraving of a beautiful nude figure, however ably executed and admired, could not be sold in America at that time. The painter, after exhibiting 'Ariadne' in New York, where no purchaser presented himself, and in need of money, disposed of it to my father for the sum of six hundred dollars. Only a recognition of the superior artistic merits of the work can explain an expenditure like that at this stage of the engraver's career! The picture, always a 'white elephant,' subject above all other mishaps to that of fire, and on that account kept stored for years in the Historical Society building, fireproof, was ultimately sold at auction for five thousand dollars, after more than thirty years' possession. Purchased by Mr. Joseph Harrison of Philadelphia, his widow afterwards presented it to the Pennsylvania Academy of the Fine Arts, where it now is.

The foregoing details, relating to the engraving period of my father's life, belong to the professional side of it ; we have now to pass on and review during this period some of the incidents illustrative of his social experiences.

CHAPTER VII.

Aspect of New York in this period—'The Lunch' Club—Out-door Painting—
Self-instruction—Affections—An Avenger of Wrong—Pseudo-reformers—
Sylvester Graham—The 'Mad Poet,' McDonald Clarke—Pupils—The
'Sketch Club' and its Objects—End of Engraving Career—Initiatory Efforts
at Painting.

THE early years of this period of my father's life may
be styled one of natural prosperity; he was happily
married, and had a home of his own, the fruit of his
talent and industry. Through an increase of income due to
bank-note engraving, he was able in 1827 to build a house in
Amity Street, then far up-town, to which he removed from
the corner of Northmoore and Hudson Streets. New York
in ten years, and notably after the completion of the Erie
Canal, had expanded prodigiously. The hills and fields
crossed by him in 1817 on his way from Grand Street to
St. Patrick's Cathedral, as mentioned in his autobiographical
sketch, no longer existed; the former had been levelled, and
the ground was now covered with monotonous red-brick
structures. In 1830, Broadway, built up to Bleecker Street,
had become a thoroughfare traversed by omnibuses. Contoit
had long established a fashionable garden near the corner
of Franklin Street, in which he enjoyed a monopoly of the
sale of ice-cream, until Niblo, in his famous garden above
Prince Street, provided the same refreshment, together with
concerts, and, finally, theatrical entertainments. No place had
existed in the city where a lady on a shopping excursion

could procure a lunch; oyster cellars alone, below the level
of the sidewalk, afforded this refreshment to men.   At
length, 'Thompson's,' in Broadway, below Park Place, supplied
the ladies with a saloon where tea, sandwiches, ice-cream,
and confectionery were to be had by anybody that appeared
to be respectable.   John Jacob Astor, in his old age, occupied
a modest, unostentatious two-story house opposite Niblo's.
On the south side of Lafayette Place 'the finest houses in
the world' were being erected, and visited on Sundays by
admiring crowds watching their progress to completion.   This
section of the city soon became the realm of fashion : 'Carroll
Place,' 'Leroy Place,' and, later on, 'Depau Row,' made
Bleecker Street its centre.   Above Amity Street came the
old 'Potter's Field,' the burial - place of the poor, then
undergoing transformation into Washington Square, still
unfenced, and with tombstones still standing there.   Beyond
the Square, on its north-eastern corner, rose a sandhill, the
property of 'Sailor's Snug Harbour,' which, soon levelled,
gave way as usual to 'splendid' houses, and especially to a
line of them nicknamed 'Presbyterian Row,' because built and
occupied by wealthy owners belonging to that Church.   After
these came scattered country houses until the House of Refuge
was reached on what is now Madison Square, and also,
outside its walls, another burial - ground, chiefly filled with
the bodies of victims to the yellow fever of 1822.   Such is
a faint glimpse of the New York landmarks of this district
in those days.   Other aspects of the city at this epoch,
vestiges of bygone characteristics, furnished by Mr. Parke
Godwin in his *Life of William Cullen Bryant*, help to
complete the picture.

'Within the city the streets were narrow, and about as dirty as they have ever since remained, but they were then frequented by loose pigs, were badly lighted by rusty oil-lamps, and poorly watched by constables in huge capes and leathern caps. . . . More compact than now, the inhabitants were generally more intimately acquainted with one another. Everybody knew everybody, and everybody took part in what was going on. The resources of enjoyment—theatres, operas, concerts, balls, and excursions—were limited; but they were open to all. Family visiting was common, so that it was easy to get into "society;" and the taverns were not so much frequented by wayfarers as by residents, to whom they answered the purpose of clubs and restaurants. Each of them, in fact, had its special circle of gossips and clever men. All the celebrities of the professions, the stage, or of literature were there to be met with; and, seated at little tables on the well-sanded floor, with pipes in their mouths and jugs of punch at their elbows, they discussed politics, books, play-actors, and the events of social life.'

A club existed at this time, founded by Cooper, the novelist, bearing the title of 'The Lunch;' the official notice to my father, advising him of his election into it, says, 'We meet at Mrs. Jones', No. 300 Broadway.' Among its members (mentioned by Mr. Godwin as belonging to the 'Bread-and-Cheese Club') were James Kent, Thomas Addis Emmett, W. D. Griffin—lawyers; Bryant, Hillhouse, Halleck, and Sands—poets; and Vanderlyn, Morse, Jarvis, and Dunlap—artists. Jarvis's humour is said by Mr. Bryant to have been 'irresistible,' as may well be imagined by the stories he told, narrated by Dunlap in his biography of that painter.

But neither prosperity nor social privileges diverted my father from his professional pursuits. His leisure hours were devoted to drawing or to painting from nature on his Hoboken rambles. For this latter purpose he set his palette before leaving his house in the city, and carried it, with a home-made easel and camp-stool, to his favourite sketching-ground. As far as I can learn, he was the first artist in the country that painted direct from nature. ' Durand had been a pioneer in engraving ; he was now a pioneer in another very important branch of study, viz., that of painting carefully finished studies directly from nature out-of-doors. Before his day our landscape-painters had usually made only pencil drawings, or, at most, slight water-colour memoranda of the scenes they intended to paint, aiding the memory by writing on the drawing hints of the colour and effect. Cole, to be sure, lived at Catskill, in full view of magnificent scenery, and was endowed with a wonderful memory, so that he gave an astonishing look of exact truth to many of his pictures of American scenery ; but he rarely, if at all, up to that period, painted his studies in the open air. Durand went directly to the fountain-head, and began the practice of faithful transcripts of "bits" for use in his studio ; and the indefatigable patience and the sustained ardour with which he painted these studies not only told on his elaborate works, but proved a contagious influence, since followed by most of our artists, to the inestimable advantage of the great landscape school of our country.' *

Other leisure hours were given as heretofore to study, as two volumes in manuscript of this date, entitled *Anatomical Notes collected while attending the Lectures of Dr. Post—* 1824, bear witness ; both contain careful drawings of parts of the human skeleton and muscular system. Another book, a pocket volume, contains notes on the study of facial expression, and still another on antique costume, the value

* *Memorial Address* by D. Huntington.

M

of which to him is apparent in the vignettes already mentioned.   He regularly attended the Drawing Societies maintained by his professional brethren, and the American Academy of Fine Arts, which possessed the collection of casts from the antique ; also the school of the National Academy of Design, in which he was both pupil and teacher. Not a moment was lost.   None of his compeers, perhaps, pursued the study of art technically with more ardour and enthusiasm.   In his eagerness to profit by added resources of all kinds, and with a family to support, and, moreover, lacking that most essential of all knowledge—the economy of one's forces—he at last broke down ; illness ensued which, together with previous poor diet during his boyhood, brought on dyspeptic troubles that never left him.   A sound constitution, however, atoned for dietetic infirmities, and this, with more exercise and less work, brought back health, as we shall see farther on.

Meanwhile, the horizon of his prosperity became clouded. Trial and sorrow, that 'grief which to man is as certain as the grave,' overtook him.   Previous to moving into his new house he lost his second child, and two years afterwards my mother declined in health, which obliged him to remove her to the highlands of New Jersey, and afterwards to Saint Augustine in Florida, where in 1830 she breathed her last. Her remains were brought back to her native place, Bloomfield, New Jersey.   This affliction obliged my father to break up housekeeping the following year.

An engraving executed at this time, exhibiting him as an avenger of wrong, may here be mentioned on account of the means employed, and the success attending its publication.   The object of it was to expose a wolf in sheep's clothing, the person in question being a clergyman, and all the more successful on that account. Better educated than ordinary men, familiar with subtleties of sentiment unknown to other corrupters, insinuating, and shielded by women, especially when a foreigner, such an individual not only finds victims more readily, but generally escapes punishment merely through dread of scandal. An experience of this kind happening to a relative led my father to warn the public against this person, and, at the same time, to secure punishment in his own way. He thought that by engraving an accurate likeness of the offender, accompanying it with a description of his character and career, and printing and circulating this throughout the country, it would track him wherever he went, and preclude further depredations. He was not mistaken, as we see in the following document and its effects :—

'This portrait is published to identify the person with the true character of one of the BASEST OF MEN.

'X......... Y......... Z.........,

a native of England, was educated a preacher in the Methodist connexion, from which he was expelled for his crimes ; afterwards he became an outlawed swindler, fled from England, leaving a wife and children, and came to the United States, where he soon married again into a respectable family, and is extensively known as a lecturer. He is classically educated and, in appearance, a gentleman, but in fact a most accomplished hypocrite. A volunteer in falsehood, none can be too base for his purpose. He abandoned his second wife without cause of complaint (which has led to the discovery of his real character and history), has swindled his best friends, violated the most sacred bonds of Honour and Affection, and, in short, is not only an Infidel in Religion but in every moral principle of Society.

'Published for the benefit of the community by A. B. Durand, New York, Dec. 8th, 1823.'

Nearly six years elapsed, when its purpose was attained, as we see in the following letter sent from Bellevue Hospital :—

'Mr. A. B. Durand,
           ' Your revenge is complete. Hunted from Boston to New Orleans, from E. to W. and from N. to S. of this northern American continent by your persecution, I now—imbecile in mind and in body, little better than a skeleton, fit only for an hospital where I may be killed or cured—call upon you to be my friend. I know and feel that my constitution of body can still be renovated. I am equally certain that the spirit which inhabits this weak frame wants only a little time when again connected with a sound body to be capable of exertion, and useful to others and honourable to itself. The fate of an immortal being is in your hands. Decide as you please. I am prepared for pardon or revenge. Persecute me to death, or give me the power of again being what you know I am capable of becoming. Imitate the God who made us both, or be the devil of men's imagination. The bearer will bring you to me.'

My father was absent, and as nothing more was heard from the offender, it is presumed that he died in Bellevue Hospital. We now turn to personages of a different stamp.

No country rivals our own in the number of its pseudo reformers, philanthropists, statesmen, and philosophers, mostly of New England origin, all, generally speaking, cherishing some pet idea or scheme which, in the so-called service of humanity, they push to extremity. An analysis of their ability may thus be formulated—one half-truth diluted in forty-nine parts of igno-rance and fifty of energy. How much good they accomplish is not always apparent ; how much mischief is known to their victims. Some are honest and innocent ; the rest are more or less stimulated by vanity, and are satisfied with acquiring a popular recognition which, they think, will hand their names down to posterity. Occasionally this belief is rewarded. The half-truth works its way, leavens the public lump, and fame compensates its promulgator. Such is the happy fate of Sylvester Graham, advocate and apostle of bran-bread. Scarcely a generation has passed since his disappearance, and his name is known not only in his own land, but in Europe, in Asia, and in Africa, wherever a dyspeptic missionary is found, and can get or make the bran-bread which assists impaired digestion. The half-truth, or theory of diet on which Graham's reputation rests, consists, summarily stated, of abstinence from animal food, coffee, tea, wine and spirits, and especially bolten flour ; in their place, people should nourish themselves on vegetables, fruits, milk, cold water, wheaten-grits, oatmeal mush, and above all, bread made of flour not deprived of its bran. Graham lectured on this theory throughout the country with enthusiasm and success. The fare of innumerable private tables was changed in conformity therewith ; meat was banished ; boarding-houses sprung up bearing his name and devoted to his system of diet ; bakers filled their ovens with bran-bread ; and influential editors, of whom Horace Greeley is a specimen, became his partisans, and enforced the theory in practice and in print. Overworked people, and especially those of sedentary occupations, changed their food and habits, took more exercise (which was probably the best detail of the theory), and benefited accordingly. My father was one of them. As he had formerly been somewhat indebted to Graham for intellectual nutriment, he accepted his physical system, and for exercise frequented the gymnasium conducted by Fuller, whose portrait he engraved. Graham and my father knew each other as early as 1812, and corresponded many years. Both, as youthful dreamers, were addicted to poetry. 'My correspondents in the city,' says Graham, in a letter of the above date, 'are very silent as to the probable success of *our* poems.' A sample of the inspiration of one of the ' poets' has already been given ; in the absence of verses by the apostle of bran-bread, the reader may judge of his poetic temperament by the following extract from the above-named letter :—

' It would indeed be ungrateful in me not to acknowledge that Nature has been bountiful in her endowments to me, but oh, how mercurial, how versatile, how strange a being has she made of me ! Serenely placid as heaven, turbulent and gloomy as hell, gentle as a lamb, extravagant as desperation, mild as the zephyr of summer, impetuous as the hurricane, kind as mercy, sanguine as a tyrant !'

Time seems to have had no effect in toning down this sort of internal ebullition. Thirteen years later he says :—

' Since I left you I have almost been in obscurity, scarcely knowing what was going on in the world, especially that part of it most interesting to me, Fine Arts and Literature ; I have been, it is true, in the neighbourhood of a college, but Heaven deliver me from such a barren soil, where every liberal feeling and cultivated taste must wither and be blighted by the mildew of ignorance, bigotry, superstition and malice. I have suffered the congregated calamities of disappointed and neglected genius and have come little short of the fate of Chatterton !'

To obtain relief, and, perhaps, recognition of his genius, he goes to Boston, the metropolis of Massachusetts :—

' I found no Academy of Arts, nor anything else in Boston worth looking at. . . . I visited Professor Everett, at his house in Cambridge, and was treated with great politeness. I read him some of my poems, and he thought that I might venture to put them in the hands of a publisher without subscription. They have tucked a ten-dollar prize on me in Boston for a poem (an " Ode to the Moon "), which I sent without knowing a prize was offered, so that I can still say that I never wrote for a prize.'

During the visit he is sadly afflicted by the death of a brother poet :—

'The news of Lord Byron's death affected me tremendously ; my spirits were exceedingly depressed ; for several weeks I could not feel reconciled to it. It seemed as though half the world were swallowed up by an earthquake, and the other half was in mourning for it. . . . I think I shall yet set the world on fire with some publications if I live !'

Fortunately for the world, circumstances did not favour the fulfilment of this intention. And yet, the half-truth Graham impressed on the minds of his contemporaries is attested by the eternal association of his name with bran-bread. As a radical change, however, in the diet of humanity, his system is a failure. But he is a sign of the times he lived in ; reformer and philanthropist, he is a passing moral and intellectual phenomenon, as with many others whose theories and predictions are falsified by knowledge and experience. Look into his mind, and we see how slight were his qualifications for the *rôle* he undertook. The only unfinished plate my father left is an unsuccessful attempt at mezzotint engraving in the portrait of his friend, Sylvester Graham.

Another character, in similar relationship at this time, is McDonald Clarke, called the 'Mad Poet.' My father befriended this eccentric personage by giving him a table in his *atelier* where he could write his letters and verses, and come and go as he pleased. He also painted his portrait, or, rather, a sketch of him. I am indebted to the Rev. Dr. L. P. Clover, then a pupil of my father's, for the following reminiscences of 'Sandy Clarke,' as the 'Mad Poet' signed his name in his correspondence.

'Poor Clarke (you must remember him, for he made your father's rooms his head-quarters), died the victim of a cruel hoax, and now lies buried in Greenwood. It may well be said of him that he had not where to lay his head. He kept a diary, which was left lying about where any visitor so disposed could peruse its contents, consisting of dreams quite amusing, and occasionally, though rarely, very indelicate, along with unfinished scraps of poetry, wild, visionary conceits, comments on books and pictures, without any idea probably that they would ever be read by anybody but himself—all recorded with a degree of faithfulness and honesty sometimes startling.

'One morning Mr. William Page, the artist, who knew Clarke well, and had doubtless heard of one of his recorded dreams, came in and asked to see the diary. It was handed to him; he read it over carefully, frowned, and, without saying a word, put it into the stove. Shortly after Mr. Page went out Mr. Clarke entered, and, looking around for his diary, complained that he could not find it. "Have you seen anything of it?" said he, addressing me. "Yes," I replied; "Mr. Page has just read it, and, being displeased with an indelicate reference to a member of his family, has burned it." "Oh," said Clarke, with the innocence of a child, "can that be possible! He should have remembered that it was only a dream." As I relinquished engraving, by advice of your father, and devoted myself to painting, Clarke afterwards sat to me for a small portrait, a rough sketch of the man on panel, but very like and characteristic. On the back of it Clarke wrote in paint the following: "Finished November 16, 1841. Clover's portrait of me is the only correct likeness ever painted. McDonald Clarke, 12 o'clock noon." *

---

* Now in the possession of Dr. Clover's son, Commander Richardson Clover of the United States Navy. The following verses are taken from a short poem composed by Clarke on the completion of the portrait :—

> ' No wonder that they think me mad,
> If mine is such a mournful face—
> So very desolate and sad—
> So furrowed with affliction's trace !
> That forehead seems like a tombstone broke
> By a midnight thunder-stroke,
> While the scant and withered hair
> Shrouds sweet hopes—wildly buried there.

'The simplicity of Clarke's nature was illustrated in nothing more fully than in the sad circumstances growing out of his painful and startling death. When I had my studio on Fulton Street, over the picture-frame store of Messrs. Greig and Campbell, opposite St. Paul's Churchyard, Clarke burst into the room one day and exclaimed, "I am going to be married." Taken by surprise I asked the name of the lady, and when the marriage was to take place. "The time is not yet definitely settled," said Clarke; "but it is coming off soon. I passed their carriage, mother and daughter together; both bowed to me very graciously. The young lady is the daughter of a well-known gentleman, president of a bank, quite wealthy; and the mother evidently, from her manner, approves of the engagement." Some young men, boarders at the Clarendon House, having heard these stories, determined, it is said, to convert the whole thing into a joke, being unable to dissuade or ridicule the subject from Clarke's mind. A letter was written, purporting to have emanated from the father of the young lady and addressed to Clarke. In this letter a high estimate was expressed for the genius and talent of Clarke, and the high honour such an alliance would be to any family, however wealthy and distinguished, adding further that he, the father of the young lady, would wish to have the wedding conducted in such style as would reflect credit upon all the parties concerned. Unwilling to offer a loan, the father of the young lady thought it would be more consistent and dignified if the prospective groom would make a note for a given time, and present it at

---

'No wonder that the women turn
Away when I have wished to wed,
And this poor heart is doomed to burn
With passions that light up the dead,
Aye, dead—for no congenial mind,
In all this cold, wide world, I find!

'Dash your brush across that brow—
Let not the far-off ages see
How sadly I am altered now;
How harsh the world has dealt with me;
How hearts that I would fain embrace
Have frown'd and darkened up that face!'

N

the bank to be cashed. Absurd as this plan was, the note was prepared and presented to the president, who, upon an explanation of the facts in the case, became very angry, pronounced the whole thing a vile imposition, and declared that no one but a madman or demented could be so imposed upon. It was a terrible blow to Clarke, who was of too sensitive a nature to rally. Rushing from the bank, the victim of a heartless joke, he was found by the watchman that night on his knees in front of St. Paul's Church, taken to a place of confinement, locked up, and there died. The next morning, when it was found that the victim was Clarke, the whole community was shocked, and the perpetrators of the cruel hoax were taught a lesson they never forgot. More than fifty years have passed since the monument erected to the memory of McDonald Clarke over his remains in Greenwood was placed where it now stands, the expense of which was contributed in part, it is said, by those who innocently, but with no less fatal than guilty consequences, engaged in the perpetration of a heartless, cruel, practical joke.'

Dr. Clover speaks of himself as a pupil of my father in the art of engraving. J. W. Casilear and two other pupils preceded him — J. W. Paradise and G. W. Hatch. Besides these, Pekenino, as we have seen, occupied a place in his *atelier*, also M. Boilly, a French stipple engraver and son of the distinguished painter of that name belonging to the French school of art of the latter part of the last century. Several applications were made by others desirous of becoming pupils, among which was that of the late John F. Kensett, the eminent landscapist. But none were accepted, as my father contemplated abandoning the practice of engraving.

'The XXI.,' or Sketch Club, demands extended notice in these pages, on account of the social influence it exercised in the development of the American school of art. It is not too much to say that the start the school obtained at this period is due to the men who belonged to this Club. The following brief history of it, abbreviated and transcribed from a paper read before the Century Club,* is here reproduced :—

In 1825 the students of art then inhabiting New York formed an association for the practice of drawing. Obtaining a room in the old almshouse building in the park, in the rear of the City Hall, in which the collection of casts imported for the American Academy of the Fine Arts had been lodged, they set up a lamp and began work devoting their evenings to it.† Out of this association sprung the National Academy of Design. Meanwhile the Annual, as described on foregoing pages, became a fashionable publication, the effect of which was to bring together artists and the literary men engaged in its preparation. An acquaintanceship sprung up between them which led to the best results. This companionship marks the incipient growth in the community of that quiet, refined, intellectual force generated by the mingling together on common ground of men of all professions, wherein, as Franklin says, 'Conversation warms the mind, enlivens the imagination, and is continually starting fresh game.' No society is better adapted to this purpose than that of artists. Their minds free of a conventional bias, indifferent to exciting questions like those of politics and business, and always observing nature, they possess a fund of ideas and experiences which, in conversation, freshen the minds of practical people with whom they come in contact, and make them excellent company. All this time the artists kept up their evening drawing - meetings. Occasionally their friends would drop in, while certain amateurs of art were invited to

* *Prehistoric Notes of the Century Club*, by J. Durand. Published by the Century Club, 1882.

† See *Annals of the National Academy of Design*, by T. S. Cummings.

join the circle, thus providing, through this pleasant intercourse, the idea of a more extended social club, which idea, then suggested, came to maturity in 1829. The object of the organization was as follows:—

1. The encouragement of social and friendly feelings among the members by occasional meetings.
2. Mutual improvement in the art which is chiefly to be practised at these meetings.
3. The production of an Annual.

The Club was of course governed by bye-laws. The first law prescribed meetings at each other's houses every Friday evening. The second prescribed sketches, the subject for which was to be selected by the entertainer, although each artist was free to choose one according to his fancy. It is recorded of one artist that 'he drew what pleased him because he was too lazy to read the poem which furnished the subject for the rest.' Regular meetings were announced in one of the daily newspapers in this cabalistic form: 'S. C.; S. F. B. M.,' indicating that the Sketch Club was to meet that evening at the house of S. F. B. Morse. These capitals seemed to have excited public curiosity, calling forth letters to the editor as to their purpose. One writer insinuated that they summoned together a gambling club. Mr. R. C. Sands, himself probably the author of the insinuation, wrote the following reply:—

'To the Editor of the " Standard."
'My Dear Sir,—I am exceedingly grieved to see by your paper of this morning that you have fallen into an enormous error respecting the nature and object of the Selebrated Cociety to which I have the honour to belong, and the existence of which is occasionally made known to the public through the press by the apparition of its formidable initials,

S. C. You appear to be somewhat alarmed at the portentous aspect of the prodigy; but, my dear friend, let me entreat you to calm your uneasiness. We S. C.'s are not gamblers, and we entertain as virtuous and laudable a horror of such iniquities as any of our fellow-countrymen. How should it be otherwise? Are we not Sober Citizens and Sincere Christians? Do we not Sleep Coundly, Sing Cheerfully, Separate Coberly, Speak Censibly, Suffer Courageously, and Sup Comfortably? You seem to think we Shuffle Cards too, but upon the Spotless Character of an S. C. it is not so; and the man who says it utters a Scandalous Calumny.

'Since you manifest so much anxiety on the subject, however, I will tell you the honest truth; we are, in fact, a Secret Combination of Sworn Conspirators; and Social Conviviality is but a Simulated Cover for the Sacred Cecrecy of our Solemn Cabal.

'Your Sensible Correspondent,

'S. C.'

The third bye-law, of a sumptuary order, and the most important, was intended to prevent extravagant entertainments, which, if tolerated, would set a bad example, defeat the object of the Club, and render it inaccessible to artists whose incomes did not warrant display of this kind. An incident occurred in this sense which shows how the overwhelming spirit of the age was exorcised for the time being, but which in after years, in the development of the Century Club, has obtained the mastery.

Tradition has it that a wealthy man found his way into the Club. As usual, a meeting took place at his house. Imagine the horror of the members when, on opening the folding-doors, a superb supper appeared before them on a table, at which they were expected to sit down. Tradition says that the members refused to do so, declaring that they would eat standing. Unfortunately for tradition a printed record of the event is extant, declaring that the members concluded to take their seats and be comfortable. Still, the honour of the Club was outraged, and it was quietly arranged to get rid of this luxurious member by dissolving the Club. No more meetings were called in the regular way. After an interval of eight months the next minutes, showing reconstruction, read as follows: 'Minutes of the Sketch Club, reorganized December 17, 1830. — At a meeting of the Sketch Club, held pursuant to notice in the Council Chamber of the National Academy of Design, it was unanimously agreed that the Sketch Club be considered extinct, and that the members present (of whom there were only five) form themselves into a committee of the whole for the purpose of organizing it anew on a more suitable plan.' A new code of laws was at once drawn up (of which there is no copy preserved), officers were elected, and the Council Chamber of the National Academy was fixed upon as the place of meeting every Friday evening; an initiation fee of five dollars was imposed, and the appointment of a caterer and treasurer restricted to one person. At the meeting held the following week the rest of the members, with the exception of the objectionable one, were present, and the Sketch Club, as it continued to the end, was finally established. In 1831 the meetings at each other's houses were resumed. It is well to notice that the title of the Sketch Club among its members was 'The XXI.,' which number was probably first fixed upon as the limit of membership. Afterwards it was extended to twenty-five.

One of the intellectual entertainments, in accordance with its purposes and attempted to be carried out, was drawing. But this did not last long. Drawing is of too absorbing a nature to allow an artist to wield the pencil and at the same time to sit still and pay no attention to the talk and laughter of those around him. Indeed, such is the verdict of the minutes, for one member is reported as complaining of ' his feelings being so much excited, and his thoughts so diverted from his subject, that for the last quarter of an hour he has been sketching nothing but peanuts and sweet-almond shells instead of " Sweet Auburn, the loveliest village of the plain." ' Frequent reference is made, again, to the publication of the Annual, an idea which did not long survive. In 1832 the following resolution was passed : ' That the Sketch Club publish a New York Annual for the year 1833, and that Mr. Durand be requested to superintend the embellishments ; also that the Corresponding Secretary be instructed to write to Mr. Verplanck (then in Congress) and request his aid in superintending the literary execution of the work.' Subsequently Messrs. Bryant, Neilson, and Emerson were appointed the literary Committee to have charge of the embryo Annual, and this is the last official record of it.

Song and instrumental music are often recorded in the minutes of the Sketch Club, while there are similar notices of stories, discussions, mirth, and philosophy. We find Mr. Bryant propounding ' a sage notion that the perfection of bathing is to jump headforemost into a snowbank.' Scientific inspiration shows itself in this question : ' Does heat expand the days in summer ?' Mr. Verplanck throws antiquarian light ' on the precise form and capacity of antediluvian butter-churns.' It would take too much space to mention every instance of Sketch Club jollity. One more example must be given on account of its novelty. In the minutes, always penned with waggish intent, it is recorded that ' a penance was imposed on Mr. Sands, Dr. Neilson, and the Secretary '—at this time

Mr. John Inman—consisting of impromptu doggerel verses, each verse to contain the word 'extract,' and 'Extract' to be the subject.

Mr. Sands began :

> ' Many elegant Extracts there be,
> Such as Syrup of Sarsaparilla ;'

Mr. Inman replies :

> ' A sort of a shrub or a tree,
> That is found in the Isles of Manilla.'

Mr. Inman again :

> ' Now, though Extracts are potent, they say
> There's no faith in the word of a woman :'

Mr. Sands :

> ' That the Extracts she makes, every way
> Are doubtful, is unknown to no man.'

Dr. Neilson :

> ' Extracting a grinder they say
> May be done with both profit and pleasure ;'

Mr. Sands :

> ' But yet there's the devil to pay
> If your gum-bone is cracked beyond measure.'

And so on until the vein runs dry.

All this belongs to the earliest years of the Sketch Club. In 1831 the members, about thirty, numbered thirteen artists, including those connected with artistic pursuits. The rest were nearly all literary men, among whom must be mentioned W. C. Bryant, John Howard Payne, and R. C. Sands, poets ; G. C. Verplanck, Hamilton Fish, Charles Fenno Hoffman, John Inman, William Emerson, Dr. Neilson, and others of literary and artistic habits and sympathies. A little later two or three lawyers of similar tastes, one merchant, and two clergymen— Rev. Drs. Dewey and Bellows—joined the Club. These men collectively may be styled the fountain-head of the subsequent prosperity of local art. At this time the public cared nothing for art, nor did any of the newspapers from an editorial point of view; the annual exhibitions of the National Academy of Design, held in the upper story of Clinton Hall, and gradually becoming the fashion, simply afforded a new public amusement, were noticed accordingly in the journals of the day, and forgotten as soon as closed. Whenever Art in other relations appealed to the public ear, at the meetings of societies or at festivals, the two clerical members of the Club acted as its spokesmen, and, besides this, they often advocated and interpreted its utility in the pulpit. The introduction into the Club of the merchant, Mr. Luman Reed, who had proved his interest in native art by a spontaneous and liberal encouragement of many of its artist members, is most significant; it marks the tendency of wealth in that direction—in brief, the support of home art by the all-powerful commercial spirit. In the next chapter the services rendered and the example set by the most eminent patron of American art will be narrated. One detail in the working of the old Sketch Club remains to be noticed, on account of the effect it produced in preventing the election of new members, and that is, the power of one black ball to exclude a candidate; it was the exclusion of members by this over-careful means that led mainly to the formation of the Century Club.

We now pass on to certain details belonging to the end of my father's career as an engraver. Successful as he had been in this profession, it must be stated that he was not fond of it. He soon discovered that he could do better. Time

o

and experience had changed his aspirations.   He found that
the world of New York was bigger than that of his father's
workshop in Jefferson Village, and that engraving afforded
only a limited field for the exercise of his artistic aptitudes.
He accordingly did not wait long to test his capacity in
other lines of art; indeed, long before the complete establishment of his reputation as engraver he began to paint as a
pastime.   The engravings of pictures by famous painters,
the knowledge of art and of celebrated artists he picked up
in a desultory manner from books and conversation, prompted
him very early to try experiments with the brush as he had
before done with the graver.   Without instruction, as in his
first attempts at engraving and when he made his own tools,
he bought a canvas, ground his colours, set his palette, and
began to paint.   His initiatory efforts—as usual with impatient
novices—seem to have been ' high art.'   As early as 1826,
according to the catalogue of the first exhibition of the
National Academy of Design, he appears before the public
with a 'Mary Magdalen at the Sepulchre;' in 1827 with
' Samson shorn of his Locks by the Philistines while asleep
in the arms of Delilah;' in 1828 with a landscape composition; in 1829, 'Hagar in the Wilderness;' and in 1831
with another 'Samson and Delilah,' when, probably because
nobody would buy these works, he abandoned this scriptural
strain altogether.   In 1832 he exhibits landscapes, and from
that time on the same class of works, together with portraits
and local historical subjects, the natural product of his talent
now finding public appreciation and patronage.   In 1833
he exhibited a portrait group of three children, which, combining figures and landscape of nearly equal interest, proved

a novelty, and, as he says in a letter to a friend, 'a very difficult task.' It was successful, however, from an artistic point of view. Two portraits were painted by him this same year : one of 'John Manesca,' a French teacher, who established the system of teaching that language afterwards pirated by Ollendorf; and another of ' Col. Aaron Ogden,' Governor of New Jersey, now in the New York Historical Society collection. These portraits brought him many commissions. Thus encouraged, he devoted himself less and less to engraving, and more and more to painting, until, finally, the former profession was entirely abandoned. He had long looked forward to this end. His labour at engraving, generally portraits, proved monotonous, while that employed on bank-note engraving, although more profitable, got to be merely mechanical drudgery. His artistic feeling would not allow him to become a mere plodder for money. It may truly be said of him that, in relation to bank-note engraving, he abandoned a fortune for love of art. Fortunately for him, as well as for the art of the country, Luman Reed appeared, and converted a mere desire to become a painter into a fixed determination. We now turn to some account of this eminent American patron of art.

CHAPTER VIII.

Luman Reed—The Service of Wealth—The Commercial Man—Early American Artists—Business Career of Mr. Reed—His Taste for Art—Our Artist visits Washington—General Jackson and his Portrait—Mr. Reed's relations with G. W. Flagg—Souvenirs of Mr. Hackett—House and Gallery of Mr. Reed —Illness and Death—Tributes by Cole, Mount, and Flagg—Effects of Mr. Reed's Example—The New York Gallery of Fine Arts.

WEALTH, in the old world derived from the people by taxation or otherwise, and disbursed by Church or State for public benefit—for Religion, Education, Charity, Science, or Art—is, in the United States, appropriated to all these civilising agencies by the 'Children of Commerce,' as Gouverneur Morris calls them; or, in other words, by private individuals who, obtaining wealth by trade or industry, solely by their own exertions, expend it *voluntarily* for public advantage. All public institutions in our country, outside of Government organization, exist directly or indirectly through the munificence of men of this stamp; all are so many monuments of a public spirit hitherto unprecedented in history. New social conditions seem to have rendered of supreme importance a hitherto subordinate force in society. To comprehend it we have only to see how the commercial man expends his wealth in gratification of his tastes and aspirations.

The motives which govern him in this respect, born out of instinct and experience rather than out of knowledge, custom, or example, are at first purely personal. Life being to him practical in the highest degree, a struggle with competitors as energetic as himself, having no time or thought to bestow on nice distinctions of fitness or propriety, his ideal aim is to get the best of everything. Of the creature comforts he must have the best, whether it be food, drink, or clothing. If he builds a house, it must be a palace ; the choicest woods and designs must be employed in its decoration, the furniture must be of the finest polish, and the curtains and carpets the richest products of the loom. A library being an indispensable adjunct to a fine house, its shelves must display the English classics along with the works of authors most in vogue, in the most elegant bindings. If pictures are bought, they are the works of distinguished foreign artists of world-wide fame, whose merit is evident by the prices their works command. Aware of the importance of culture, his children must enjoy the great advantages their father lacked, and must go to the best and dearest schools ; with respect to religion, his family must attend a fine church with an eloquent preacher, and occupy the best pew in it.* Ideals of this stamp are to be gratified materially and rapidly.

But the intellect of the commercial man is not thus limited ; he cherishes nobler ideals and acts under higher impulses. Personal longings being satisfied, he concerns himself with the welfare of society. His sympathies are warm and active. Crime, misery, suffering, poverty, and disease are evils always apparent that need no special study ; he belongs to societies for the repression of crime, superintends and founds every sort of hospital and asylum. Fully sensible of the value of religion to

---

* 'In securing precedence in the house of the Lord, the control of money superseded age and recognition of private worth, or public service, or family consideration.'—*Three Episodes in Massachusetts History*, by Charles Francis Adams, page 38.

society, he assists congregations of all sects in the building of churches. Knowing the value of superior instruction, he founds technical schools, great libraries and universities, all of which come within the scope of common sympathies without regard to culture. When culture is requisite, as in the case of art, the munificence of the commercial man is less significant ; personal in his aims, his expenditure is lavish for the decoration of his dwelling, but for the benefit of the public in art his largess is more limited than that bestowed in other directions. The Corcoran Gallery in Washington, with its ample revenue exclusively devoted to the formation of a free public gallery, is thus far the sole institution organized by a private individual for purposes growing out of wide culture in art.

With the foregoing for a preface, we now turn to Luman Reed, whose name is placed at the head of this chapter, a man scarcely known beyond his generation, and who, a superior type of amateur, may be said to have prepared the way for this order of progress. After acquiring a fortune by untiring energy, he affords a remarkable example of intelligence and generosity in the use of it. Before setting forth the character and influence of Mr. Reed, it is necessary to revert briefly to the state of art in the country before he came upon the stage.

American art in the eighteenth century and first years of the nineteenth, as far as it can be shown by works produced on our soil, begins with Smybert, a Scotch painter born in Edinburgh in 1684, and induced to come to this country by Dean Berkeley in 1728. Smybert settled and married in Boston, where he painted portraits. His principal work, a picture of the family of Dean Berkeley, is now in New Haven. The talent of Smybert was not of the first class. In any event, it was sufficiently great to

LUMAN REED.

Reproduced from the Portrait in the possession of Frederick R. Sturges, Esq.
Heliogravure Dujardin. Printed by C. Wittmann.

attract young students of art, and serve them as a sort of educator. Among those who profited by a study of his work were Copley, Trumbull, and Allston. John Singleton Copley, born in Boston, 1738, began to paint spontaneously at a very early age. 'Pieces executed by him in Boston, before (to use his own words) he had seen any tolerable picture, and certainly before he could have received any instruction from the lips of a master, show his natural talent.'* His principal works, painted in America before 1776, when he went to England and finished his career, consist of portraits. In this branch of art he produced some not afterwards excelled by him, of which two now in the possession of Mr. Martin Brimmer, of Boston, attest the importance. He acknowledges his indebtedness to the works of Smybert. Charles Wilson Peale, born in Maryland, 1741, comes next in order. He visited Copley in Boston, in 1768, who 'afforded him great enjoyment and instruction.' In 1770 he went to London and became a pupil of West's. On returning home, in 1774, he practised portrait-painting during revolutionary times as well as in after years. Then comes Gilbert Stuart, the most remarkable of all, and, as a portrait-painter, still without a rival. Malbone, born in 1794, whose miniatures equal those of any painter, was an American. Wertmuller, a Swede who came to this country in 1794, and died here in 1872, an artist of great ability, and Robert Edge Pine, born in England, complete the list of artists of superior merit whose works are conspicuous in the early stages of the American school. Of Trumbull we have already spoken.

Portraiture, accordingly, was the only branch of art that met with any spontaneous encouragement, and that enabled

* Dunlap, *History of the Arts of Design in the United States.*

a local artist with a family to support himself. The absorbing
cares of life at this purely practical stage of the nation's
growth prevented the indulgence of ideal aspirations ; nobody,
consequently, desired to possess a work by a home artist other
than a portrait of a relation, or of some real or fancied great
man of the day.   Certain artists, like Peale and Trumbull,
painted pictures to please themselves, but at their own risk
and always without adequate compensation.   Dunlap, in his
History of the Arts of Design in the United States, in which
he narrates the lives and fortunes of American artists down to
1833, records only a few exceptions to this rule. These facts
prove not the lack of talent, but a state of public culture that
afforded no encouragement for art beyond that of depicting
the features of a man or a woman.   All native-born artists
capable of doing better work, and free of, or indifferent to,
money restrictions, emigrated to Europe—West, Copley, Stuart
(more of an adventurer than the rest), Newton, Leslie, Allston,
and Vanderlyn—where they studied, and obtained recognition
and honour.   West became President of the Royal Academy,
Leslie the recipient of royal favour, Allston a celebrity of the
day as painter and poet, and Vanderlyn a competitor of French
artists, and awarded a medal.   Stuart, Allston, and Vanderlyn,
it is true, returned home.   Allston brought with him a reputation acquired abroad that reflected honour on his country, but
he lived and died in Boston in comparative poverty.   Vanderlyn
on his return went back to his native village, Kingston, on the
Hudson River, and lived there almost unknown ; in any event,
he wore out a vexed and broken spirit in the vain effort to
secure a foothold in an unsympathetic community, obtaining
recognition only when his powers had failed.   Both were artists

of capacity, but their art was grafted on the grand old stock of European thought and feeling. Stuart, devoted wholly to portraiture, found appreciation in both countries, and was successful. We now turn to Luman Reed, the first wealthy and intelligent connoisseur who detected and encouraged native ability in other directions than in portraiture.

Luman Reed was born in 1785, in a village called Green River, Columbia County, State of New York. In his boyhood he removed to Coxsackie, a small town on the Hudson River about twenty-five miles below Albany, where he was educated at the expense of an uncle in an ordinary school. When old enough he entered a country store at Coxsackie, and subsequently became the partner and brother-in-law of his employer. During this period of his life he acted as a sort of supercargo on a sloop called the *Shakespeare*, belonging to the firm, and plying between Coxsackie and New York, the voyage commonly lasting ten days. His functions consisted in selling the produce of the farms around Coxsackie, and in purchasing goods in New York for his country store. Finding by experience of this kind that New York offered a larger field for the exercise of his abilities, he at length left the country, and, carrying with him the little capital he had accumulated, became a merchant on a larger scale in that city. This 'start in life,' it may be added, is that of thousands of young Americans of similar energy and foresight.

The details of Mr. Reed's business career need not be dwelt on; it is necessary only to note the qualities which ensured his success—sagacity, promptness, self-reliance, remarkable organizing power, and strict discipline in relation to his subordinates, accompanied with great solicitude for their

P

interests and welfare. Two or three trifling occurrences illustrate these characteristics. On one occasion he had purchased
forty hogsheads of sugar, and told his carman that he was to
bring them to the store in the afternoon. Meanwhile he had
resold them. On returning to his place of business he tells
the carman: 'I sold that sugar and made one hundred and
fifty dollars by it, but I saved you the cartage.' At another
time he bought a lot of wine and sent the carman for it.
The seller, having had no time, probably, to ascertain his
credit, refused to deliver it, and sent back a note to that
effect. 'Where is the wine?' demanded Mr. Reed. 'I got
only this note,' replied the carman. Mr. Reed opened the
note and read it. 'Tell him,' he exclaimed, 'my endorser is
in my pocket. If he has any of my notes, send them here
and I'll cash them. Stop! I'll go with you!' He jumped
on the cart, and 'I tell you,' said the carman, 'I had to
hurry.' In ten minutes his credit was established and the
wine delivered. One morning the clerk whose duty it was to
open the store very early in the morning overslept the cus-
tomary hour; on reaching the store he found 'L. Reed,
5 o'clock,' in chalk on the door. The sentinel was not at
his post on the rounds of the general, and this was the mode
of punishment. His was the discipline of soldiers who feel
that the general is ever present, but at the same time who
know that he is always considerate. Everybody under him,
up to the day of his death, almost worshipped him. It only
remains to say that, in the commercial world, which is a great
battle-field, Mr. Reed was an accomplished strategist, and made
good use of victory.

Between 1815 and 1832, a period of seventeen years, a

fortune rewarded Mr. Reed for his toil. He now began to gratify other instincts, not rooted in gain. Art seems to have attracted his attention spontaneously. As usual with commercial men whose natural tastes are kept in abeyance by the exigencies of business, his first impulse was to possess the best works of art that could possibly be had, which in those days consisted of 'Old Masters,' the æsthetic standards of the time. He accordingly resorted to 'Michael Paff, Esq.,' the only accredited authority and dealer in pictures in New York, who supplied him, in commercial phraseology, with 'the best the market could afford.' How many Mr. Reed bought is not known. Very soon, however, he discovered he was purchasing counterfeit 'goods,' and he got rid of his acquisitions in much less time than it took to buy them. Abandoning 'Michael Paff, Esq.,' he trusted to his own tastes and sympathies. At this time the exhibitions of the National Academy of Design, held in Clinton Hall, Nassau Street, and then becoming attractive, presented an art which he could comprehend, consisting of subjects derived from local life, history, and scenery. He sought the acquaintance of the artists who furnished them, and at once interested himself in their labours. Finding them co-workers like himself on an entirely new field, it is probable that his sympathy for their efforts was quickened by this fact. However this may be, he availed himself of the opportunity to procure original productions. His first commission, in 1834, was given to my father. The following documents narrate their subsequent intercourse and the beginning of an encouragement of native art that led to most important results.

In 1835 Mr. Charles Augustus Davis, author of the famous political letters by 'Major Jack Downing,' commissioned my

father to visit Washington and paint a portrait of Henry
Clay, then Senator from Kentucky and the great opponent of
the policy of General Jackson, who occupied the presidential
chair.   Mr. Reed at the same time commissioned him to paint
the portrait of General Jackson.   In fulfilment of these commissions the artist writes from Washington, February 28th,
1835: 'I obtained an introduction to Mr. Clay, made known
my business, and was assured by him that he could not sit for
his portrait, ... his time being entirely taken up by the
pressure of business at the close of Congress. . . . I have
learned nothing relating to the portrait of the President, having
to dance attendance on "great men" two or three days before
one can get an answer to a simple question. . . . If I cannot
begin this week I shall give up the business, and, like Jack
Downing, "turn my back on the White House until I'm sent
for."'

On the 12th of March he reports: 'For a whole fortnight I have been able to obtain only two sittings of the
President. . . . Since writing the above I have had another
half-sitting, but under such unfavourable circumstances that I
fear I shall not be able to satisfy myself : he smokes, reads,
and writes, and attends to other business while I am painting,
and the whole time of a sitting is short of one hour ; but all
say that I have an excellent likeness ; . . . . however, it is
not good enough to satisfy me.   The General has been part
of the time in a pretty good humour, but sometimes he gets his
"dander up" and smokes his pipe prodigiously.'

And not only that, but, as my father related on returning
home, he could overhear the President, at the meetings of his
Cabinet in the adjoining room, warmly disputing with the

members of it and vociferating ' by the Eternal !' together with less temperate expletives, in the most energetic manner ; on entering to give a sitting, and obliged to sign papers on his knee as these were constantly brought in, he would denounce Henry Clay in unmeasured terms.

Meanwhile Mr. Reed extended his commission so as to include portraits of all the Presidents of the United States up to that day. He writes :—

' I intend to make presents of them to one of our public institutions of Science and Natural History. . . . It is not proper for me to mention the name of the institution until the presentation is made. . . . If possible, get that of the Hon. John Quincy Adams [then in Washington], also Jefferson, from an original by Stuart, and likewise Monroe. . . . I forgot the portrait of the genuine patriot, John Adams, which I hope you will consent to copy for me, be it where it may. . . . Washington and Madison you already have.'

In 1832 my father had painted a portrait of the venerable ex-President Madison, at his residence in Virginia, for George P. Morris, editor of the *New York Mirror*. The execution of Mr. Reed's commission at this time involved an excursion to Boston, soon after the return of the artist to New York. The following extracts from his letters narrate his occupation and experiences there. Mr. Reed accompanied him. He writes, June 10th, 1835 :—

' I have been at work to some account since I wrote last, but, gadding about and looking at everything in and out of Boston most of the time, I have of course not made much progress, although I have four pictures begun ; one of a beautiful little girl, the grand-daughter of Mr. Adams, which I paint at the request of Mr. Reed, to be presented to Mr. Adams ; another, a portrait of the Hon. Edward Everett for Mr. Davis (Major Jack Downing), who gave me the order soon after my arrival here ; and a third, the head of President John Adams (after Stuart), which is almost done, as well as that of John Quincy Adams, an entirely new portrait from life, and much better than the one I did in Washington. I shall begin copies of Washington and his wife immediately. After Mr. Reed leaves me I shall have nothing to do but work and make the most of my time. I have dined once with Mr. Adams, and have promised to do so again to-morrow. His residence is eight miles from Boston, which renders it not so convenient as I could wish for sittings in taking his and his grand-daughter's portraits. But as I have already said, no inconvenience shall interfere in my carrying out the wishes of Mr. Reed, who seems to think of nothing else while here but to promote my best interests. You will smile to know that he assures me I shall yet ride in my own carriage. If I am ever able only to paint as well as he hopes and flatters himself that I will, I shall care but little for a carriage provided I continue able to walk and to work.'

On returning to New York, Mr. Reed writes the following letter, showing in what way he facilitated the painter in accomplishing his work :—

'NEW YORK, *June* 15, 1835.

'You will no doubt be a little surprised to see Mr. Allen [his son-in-law] back in Boston again so soon. He is going to finish up what he left undone ; he will tell you what he is after. I have this morning seen Mr. Gouverneur, son-in-law of Mr. Monroe, and he informs me that Stuart's original of Mr. Monroe is at Baltimore, in the hands of Mr. Rogers, and that the portrait at Oak Hill is by Sully. I have seen the one in his mother's possession by Vanderlyn, which is very well painted. Mr. Gouverneur says that it is the best likeness, except that in the possession of S. E. Burrows, by Paradise, which you are familiar with. . . . I am told by Mr. Gouverneur that the original of Madison by Stuart is at Oak Hill. It seems to be a difficult thing to find out where the originals of Madison and Monroe really are. You could tell them if you could set eyes on them.'

Knowing my father's interest in the National Academy, he adds :—

'The exhibition at the Academy comes on very well. Over $1900 has been taken in, and the receipts will be at least $2000 by the close. I hope to hear that you are getting on to your mind, of which I have no doubt. Mr. Sturges is anxious for your return. I think he wants you to paint both of his children. Wishing you health, happiness, and fame, 'I am, yours sincerely,

'LUMAN REED.'

Writing a few days later to his friend and pupil, Mr. Casilear, my father narrates his visit to Washington Allston :—

'I have seen everything in art and nature that the place affords, and there is much worth seeing. The most interesting object to me is our country's greatest painter. We have paid him two visits. He is indeed an interesting personage. I cannot but regret that he declines Mr. Reed's request to paint a picture for him on account of the necessary time ; he has promised, however, to do so as soon as his present engagements are fulfilled, among which is the finishing of " Belshazzar's Feast," which he intends soon to unroll. He expressed a great desire to see my print of " Ariadne." Having brought an impression to Boston with me, I was able to gratify him, and if I had not become in some measure insensible to the tickling of praise on that point, I should be fully satisfied with the high compliments he paid me. He wishes some conversation with me before I leave on engraving his picture of the " Bloody

Hand." At an earlier period of my life this would have given me the highest satisfaction ; now it comes with less relish. Still, could I obtain assistance on the subordinate parts, I should be willing to undertake it for the sake of doing some work by so distinguished an artist. I expect a visit from him soon, when I shall be obliged to undergo the ordeal of submitting my painting to his eye, for the result of which I am a little more anxious.'

What this opinion was does not appear—it is doubtful if it was flattering, considering the aim, attainments, and technical proficiency of the two artists. The admiration of the younger artist for the genius of his superior was nevertheless then great, and remained undiminished after years of experience and an opportunity to compare his works with those of the great European masters. The following passage in the same letter is given as a passing comment. Speaking of an exhibition in Boston, my father says :—

'There are three works by Allston in it, two portraits and the other a single figure of a "Troubadour," which I think you would pass by without notice. I have seen others in this city by him which I cannot appreciate ; but there are some which cannot be misunderstood—one, a landscape, I think equal in colour, light and shade, to anything I ever saw.'

On the 2nd of June he writes :—

'I am getting homesick. But the remedy will be at hand in one week more, for I begin to see through my labours. If nothing interferes I shall close, or very nearly so, this week. My work has been nearly double what I expected. Since I wrote last I have begun another portrait from life, the father-in-law of Mr. Everett and of Mr. C. F. Adams (son of John

Quincy Adams), for whom I am painting it. All pronounce my likenesses " first-rate." But, however, flattering their good opinions and the commissions given me may be, I still hope that I may not be induced to undertake others, for I wish to be at home, and to that end every hour of the day is devoted to the completion of what I have in hand. I have finished six heads and have three more far advanced—in all, nine portraits, five of which are originals and the others copies for Mr. Reed. This is the amount of my labour, and if I finish this week, I shall have done the whole in three weeks—which is not slow.'

Some might think too fast—that the quality of the work was endangered by speed. But, considering that the painter was plying his brush every hour of daylight, the rate of speed may be accepted. Evidence of how he employed himself, as well as a glimpse of his abstemious and other habits, may be gathered from the following passage at the end of the above letter :—

'Since Mr. Reed left I have lived in complete solitude, working all day in my painting-room and passing the evening in my bedroom. At table we have three or four ladies, as many gentlemen, and sundry children, yet they are about as silent as ours at home. As for myself, I say little—drink coffee and green tea regularly because there is none other. I eat dyspepsia bread, which is not " Graham " bread in Boston, together with whatever else comes before me, being noways particular—so you may conclude that I am not sick, otherwise than homesick. I have had a good many of what are called luxuries since I have been in Boston, and have drunk more champagne and other wines than for a year past in New York; yet I would by far prefer a crust of Graham bread and black

tea at home to them all.   Yet I foresee that this excursion
will amply compensate me for all the inconvenience which it
occasions.'

The series of portraits of the Presidents, ordered by Mr.
Reed, was presented by him to the Museum and Library in
the Navy Yard, Brooklyn.   Another series, duplicates, were
kept by him for his own gallery, of which more will be said
further on.   I note here a passage in one of Mr. Reed's letters
addressed to my father in Washington : —

'The all-absorbing subject of my letters of yesterday and the day
before occupied my mind so much that I did not even mention my
portrait that you painted for Mr. Sturges. He has got it home and it
is hung up ; it stands the test of the critics ; even Paff says that it is
first-rate, and he, you know, spares nobody but the old masters.'

Early in the previous year, 1834, Mr. George W. Flagg,
a young man who had just made his *début* in the art world,
had produced several remarkable works which attracted Mr.
Reed's attention.   Recognising his talent and wishing to afford
a young beginner every educational facility, he at once adopted
him, as it were, and sent him to Europe, defraying all his
expenses.   The spirit which animated Mr. Reed—his solicitude,
moral and material, for those he helped, his views of art and
comments on it, which, if not always learned, are at least
original and to the point—is apparent in the following letter
to Mr. Flagg, dated March 9th, 1835 :—

'MY DEAR MR. FLAGG,
        'I was quite delighted on receiving your letter, as it was the
first intimation of your arrival in Paris. You say you like Paris better
than London. I am much pleased to hear you denounce* the French

---

* In the sense of criticise.

school of painting; pure, simple nature is the school, after all. You left here with a good idea of the general tone of colour, and I hope it may never be corrupted. You say you have become a great admirer of Paulo Veronese as well as Titian. I hope to see your execution as good as theirs some day. You have more to do than you are now aware of to satisfy your admirers in this country; your fame stands higher here than any young artist's ever did at your age, and to keep pace with expectation will require all the efforts you can muster. I hope you will not turn off a picture until the work is masterly executed; one picture finished in that way will be of more service to you than fifty that lack detail. You know my motto, " With application comes everything." I really look to you to give a spur to art in this country—not by startling objects, gorgeous colouring, and a thousand incongruities to catch the eye of the vulgar, but by boldness of design, truth in expression, and simple arrangement of figures and colouring that shall bring out nature itself to view. Execution is an important point; a cat well painted is better than a Venus badly done. My pride is at stake in your success, and you must not disappoint me. . . . It is important to learn to judge correctly of your own works; the opinions of most people will only be to flatter you, so little does the world care about real friendship ! Compare your works with Titian's, as if both were his, and then judge which is best. I bought a picture a few days ago by one of the old masters, Fyt, the subject " Dogs and Game," the size of life, a first-rate specimen of the art* and I must say that I never knew what could be done in painting before. The subject I do not admire, but as a work of art it is first-rate. I am now a believer in the old masters. You say that you should like to have me slip over to Paris and go with you to Florence. I should like it much, and some day or other I intend to travel over the ground and shall want you to go with me. Would you not derive more advantage by constant practice in Paris during your present stay in Europe, and then visit Italy after you have become more perfect in the art ? I expect you to come back much improved, because I think you have a mind for it. But I am sorry to say that improvement has not

---

* This work, probably genuine, is now in the collection of Mr. Reed's pictures, preserved in the New York Historical Society building.

been the result with most of the artists that have gone to the continent for
that purpose ; they have come back with the exalted notion of having
seen great works ; have looked, talked, and travelled away their time, and
come back more ignorant than when they went away. These instances
are familiar to you. They did not stick down in a place and apply themselves. The art is not lost, talent is not deficient, nor is encouragement
of merit wanting. I have set my heart on your success. I have boasted
of your talent and of your great moral worth, and everybody that knows
you looks forward to great things. I fear not the allurements of Paris.
I know that your mind is above them. Fame is before you, but be
careful that you do not overrate yourself ; self-sufficiency is certain ruin.
. . . . I want you to copy the likeness of Claude in the Louvre ; I want
the portrait to hang up. I also want you to make for me drawings in
crayon of three of the best antique statues in the Louvre. Wishing you
health and happiness, I am your most

' Devoted friend,

' Luman Reed.'

Two months later Mr. Reed writes to my father in
Boston :—

' I am quite happy in being identified with you in your visit to Boston,
and I hope we may often be identified together, if my being so will
promote your interest and success in this naughty world. My young
friend Flagg has returned from Europe brimful of enthusiasm ; he says that
America is the place for him and he wants no better nature than we have
to study from. Now I like this. Let us make something of ourselves
out of our own materials and we shall be independent of others. It is all
nonsense to say that we have not got the material. . . . I hope your
admirers in Boston will not draw off your attachment from New York, as
we cannot think of giving you up. . . . I shall be glad to see you back.
. . . . You are now, in my opinion, fairly under way in your new
profession, and I believe your success is certain.'

Mr. Reed's benefactions were not confined to painters.
Long before the period in which the foregoing letters were
written he had for a business neighbour a man who, through

his aid, became a distinguished American artist in another branch of art, Mr. James H. Hackett, the well-known actor, living at a time when histrionic genius was more abundant and better understood than at the present day. Mr. Hackett, then a merchant occupying a warehouse alongside of Mr. Reed's, was remarkable for his comic stories; in the dull hours of the business season he often dropped in on his neighbours and entertained them with his humour. Unsuccessful in business, he went on the stage at Mr. Reed's suggestion.

' I found,' says Mr. Hackett, ' upon the occasion of my *début* at the Park Theatre, over four hundred of the first merchants of New York, gathered and induced thither by my business neighbour, Mr. Reed, to afford me their countenance. He sought an interview repeatedly by calls at my home and importuned me to acquaint him with my condition, and to permit him to use his influence with my few creditors, each a personal friend of his, to effect a compromise.'

Continuing the story in another letter Mr. Hackett adds, writing to his friend Mr. Charles M. Leupp :—

' My intimacy with that honest, industrious, single-hearted, simple-mannered, liberal-handed, and generous-minded philanthropist—one of the most modest, energetic, cordial, sincere, disinterested, and unostentatious of Nature's nobility—originated, as you have heard me describe, in 1825-6, soon after my mercantile bankruptcy, when he unexpectedly and spontaneously, by his counsel and influence, and the temporary loan of a thousand dollars (to add to some three thousand I had made within a few weeks by adopting the stage in my despondency), relieved me from my liabilities to my creditors, and enabled me to extend the sphere of my new professional pursuits to other cities and countries without fear of molestation. " I thought, Hackett," said he, " if you were convinced by the personal countenance of some of the oldest merchants of New York, and which I could influence in your favour, that, though you had unfortunately lost your credit as a merchant, you still had, as a man, the respect of the community, you would be less endangered by your new associations of losing your own." As long as he lived he gave me his friendship, confidence, and social countenance in this community, each timely and of incalculable advantage. God knows how warmly I appreciated not only his persevering benefactions, but the pure, Christian-like motives which originally inspired his interference. My spirit seemed to him broken by my fortunes in trade, and which, neglected then, he feared might lead to loss of self-respect, carelessness of the opinion of the world, and consequent inability as well as unfitness to educate and furnish my three sons (three, five, and six years old), with a fair start on approaching manhood. When Mr. Reed, surprising me by his offer to try and succour my distress, mentioned that money would be necessary to add to what I had just earned in order to free me from my debts, some of them being in suit, and specified one thousand dollars, I inquired, " But how and when am I to obtain such an additional sum sooner than a few months hence, and from my new profession in which I am hardly embarked, whereas it must be had next week?" Mr. Reed instantly replied, " I will lend it to you. And that you may still feel yourself free I will not take a scrap of paper in acknowledgment of the loan, nor mention it to my partner, my family, nor to any one. Call any day you please and I will hand you a bank-note." '

The loan was made and the money refunded in a couple of months. Mr. Hackett adds :—-

' From the many acts of a similar nature which were done in secret by him, but detected after his too-early death, he must absolutely have gone about seeking opportunities for his benefaction, and earned many earthly blessings from the recipients of his bounty. But, if it should be asked, " What has such an incident to do with Fine Arts?" Answer, "Much— the Pen aiding the Pencil to delineate the mental with the facial features, and thus illustrate Humanity." '

The foregoing documents suffice to give the reader a good idea of Mr. Reed's relations with artists in gratifying his noblest instincts, as well as of his influence in fostering their interests with the public. Further evidence of all this is found in his encouragement of other contemporary artists whose works he appreciated, and whose careers interested him to the same extent. His relations with Thomas Cole, the most prominent landscapist of his day, were equally intimate and fruitful. Mr. Cole, of English birth, came to the United States at a very early age, but afterwards returned to Europe, where his mind, impressed by the phenomena of old-world development in contrast with that of the new world just starting in civilisation, conceived the idea of pictorially describing the 'Course of Empire,' as visible in the five stages of its secular growth—birth, progress, grandeur, decline, and end in ruin. The series of pictures painted by him begins with a landscape view, preserved throughout the series, in which we observe successively primitive life in the dawn of day; social progress in the morning hours; architectural splendour, and the processional pageantry of imperial dominion in the full glare of noonday; war, conquest, and destruction in the decline of day; and, finally, utter ruin at evening in the pale light of a rising moon, where naught that indicates empire remains on the landscape but a solitary column and the ineffaceable landmarks of nature. On Mr. Cole mentioning to Mr. Reed that he would like to paint such a subject, Mr. Reed told him to fix his price and go on with it. Mr. Cole named two thousand five hundred dollars, which sum Mr. Reed afterwards, on seeing the labour involved, voluntarily increased to four thousand five hundred dollars, besides giving the artist all the advantages of the exhibition of his work. Its effect on the public was very great, and notably in increasing the number of appreciators of native art. Among them may be mentioned Mr. Samuel Ward, who, later on, commissioned Mr. Cole to paint 'The Voyage of Life,' a similar series, and subsequently engraved by Mr. James Smillie.

Next comes W. S. Mount. This young artist began his career in 1828, with, as usual, a Scripture subject, the 'Raising of the daughter of Jairus.' Again, as usual, nobody took a fancy to this picture and bought it. The following year he tempted the public with still another subject of the same class, 'Saul and the Witch of Endor,' and, at the same time, descending the imaginative scale of ideas, 'Crazy Kate' and 'Celadon and Amelia,' both pictures meeting with the same fate. Finally, in 1830, after falling back on portraiture, in which he was more successful, Mount produced 'The Rustic Dance after a Sleigh-ride,' showing his powers on the humorous side of American rural life and the admiration of which by the public established his artistic position. In 1834 Mr. Reed and Mount became acquainted, and in 1835 we find him the owner of Mount's two masterpieces, 'Bargaining for a Horse' and 'Unruly Boys,' exhibited in 1836. After this Mount was never without a commission.

Mr. Reed's encouragement of the artist's efforts at portraiture, which led him to abandon engraving entirely, have been set forth. Meanwhile, having already painted one historical subject as early as 1833, which was exhibited in 1835 and soon disposed of ('The Capture of Major André'), my father, ambitious of pursuing art in that direction, painted for Mr. Reed 'The Wrath of Peter Stuyvesant' and 'The Pedler,' the latter a picture of local life suggested by Wilkie's treatment of similar subjects. In painting 'The Capture of Major André' he conferred with Mr. J. K. Paulding, a descendant of one of the captors, in relation to costume and historical points, visited

THE WRATH OF PETER STUYVESANT.

'On receiving these direful tidings (the taking of Fort Casimir) the valiant Peter started from his seat—dashed the pipe he was smoking against the back of the chimney—thrust a prodigious quid of tobacco into his left cheek—pulled up his galligaskins, and strode up and down the room.' — *A History of New York, from the Beginning of the World to the End of the Dutch Dynasty*, by Diedrich Knickerbocker.

Reproduced from the Original Picture, belonging to the Collection of the
New York Gallery of Fine Arts, in the possession of the New York Historical Society.
Heliogravure Dujardin. Printed by C. Wittmann.

the spot near Tarrytown where André was arrested, and, in the figures, had the advantage of depicting personages whose cast of feature and character were familiar to him. The picture is accordingly a complete expression of his powers in this line of art. Subsequently engraved, the figures by Alfred Jones and the landscape by James Smillie, distributed over the country by the American Art Union, often copied on signs and in other rude ways, it seems to have become the standard representation of the subject. In the ' Wrath of Peter Stuyvesant,' imaginary in all respects, he invents characters and accessories. The humour of the scene, which is of most consequence artistically, cannot be mistaken. The ire and energy of the old Dutch governor, in contrast with the patient attention of the dumpy and rubicund trumpeter, Anthony van Corlaer, and the fright of the tall half-breed Indian, leave little to be desired. As early attempts in an historical line, these works cannot be over-looked in the history and development of national art. Other works of the same order will be noted farther on. All that now remains in completing this chapter is to narrate the closing circumstances of Mr. Reed's career.

As usual with the typical commercial man, Mr. Reed, on becoming wealthy, built a fine house in the lower part of the city. But it was not a palace. On the contrary, his residence, in style of architecture and the arrangement of the interior, conformed to the habits and mode of life of his contemporaries, and differed from other dwellings only in being more com-modious and better constructed, the materials being of the very best quality and the mechanics employed ' the best that money could procure.' One feature of it that made it unique was an upper story devoted to a collection of paintings pro-

R

cured, in the main, during the erection of the house, and for which Mr. Reed had made no provision on laying its foundations. In any event, the third story, before the house was finished, was adapted to the purposes of a picture-gallery, as well as this could be done without a skylight in the roof. When the building was completed the pictures were duly hung. During this operation it occurred to Mr. Reed that the effect of the gallery would be improved by painting the doors, all of them blank spaces among the pictures, in harmony with the general tone of colour which prevailed on the walls. Accordingly he commissioned Cole, Mount, Flagg, and my father, whose works were suspended there, to execute designs in this sense. In this connexion, as well as giving one of Mr. Reed's judicious observations on the art which he called into being, the following letter to Mr. Flagg, dated December 30th, 1835, may be cited :—

'I look for you about the first of the month, and shall expect you to stay with me some time and paint in the gallery. The life-school is open at the Academy, and you can avail yourself of that if you wish. Mount has painted another picture for me, which, in some parts, shows a perfection in the art which I did not expect to see so soon from any one. I do not believe that Ostade or Teniers ever did anything better than some parts of the picture.'

Another detail of this gallery must be recorded—it was open one day in the week to visitors. This circumstance, the first of its kind, and that of the decoration of the gallery, simple facts in themselves, indicate both the unconventional way in which Mr. Reed carried out his plans, as well as his ability and disposition to foster the growing interest of the public in art.

The foregoing narration, it is hoped, gives a clear idea of the character of this eminent commercial man and patron of American art. The following account of the illness which terminated his career in the prime of life shows the appreciation of him by the artists whom he had so sympathetically and nobly befriended. Mr. Reed and my father in the spring of 1836 were to have visited Mr. Cole, who lived at Catskill. Instead of going, however, my father thus writes to Mr. Cole under date of May 12th, 1836 :—

'I am sorry to say that we are prevented from paying you the promised visit by the sickness of Mr. Reed. He was taken very violently the morning you left, and the first favourable appearances are to-day. . . . His disease is said to be remittent fever with inflammation of the liver. I have not seen him since he was taken down, and although it is not yet three days it has seemed to me like weeks, so heavily and painfully has the time passed. I doubt not that you will look with the same anxiety as myself to the happy moment of his recovery. God grant that it may not be long. I will not trouble you with the many melancholy reflections that have come over me during the short interval since parting from you, and only say that I will write again in a few days if Mr. Reed is not able to write you himself.'

Three days later, adding a postscript, he says: 'By keeping this letter till this morning I am able to add a bit more of comfort. I have just been to Mr. Reed's and find him considerably better; and although I would be cautious in indulging in joyful feeling, I cannot but feel a little lightened of a grievous burden, so much so that I could scarcely keep from singing aloud as I returned up Broadway to add this postscript for you. . . . You know, my dear friend, that I alone am not an interested individual in this matter. I dare not think on the desolation that his loss would occasion.'

On the 20th of May he reports that the patient is better, but unable to sit up 'in consequence of the great prostration of the system by profuse bleeding.' May 25th, he adds, 'I have at length had the pleasure of seeing our friend for the first time on Sunday, and again to-day. . . . He desires to be particularly remembered to you, thinks of you constantly, and says that it is his greatest satisfaction to know that he has such good friends. Could I find words to express the interest I feel, for one, in that friend, I would attempt it, but your own heart will best conceive it. Suffice it to say that, although taught by experience to be cautious of enjoyments proceeding from attachments of the heart, having suffered all the agony of bereavement, I still find myself so deeply attached to him that the very thought of his loss fills me with a gloom and sadness which almost unfits me for the common duties of the day.'

One more letter is dated June 7th, 1836 :—

'The fatal hour has come. Our dear friend is dead. The funeral will take place on Thursday afternoon. Come and look for the last time on the man whose equal we never shall see again. I can say no more.

'Yours in deepest sorrow,

'A. B. DURAND.'

On learning the sad intelligence from my father, Mr. Mount writes :—

'I have received your letter of the 11th inst., informing me of the death of our best friend, Mr. Luman Reed. The more I think of him, the more sorrowful I feel that he is taken away from us. How pleasing he was in his address! How well he understood the feelings of the artists! He was one we shall always love to remember.'

Mr. George W. Flagg expresses like sentiments, adding,—

'He was indeed a father to me, ever ready to cheer me on; and often, by his counsel and affectionate encouragement, has he imparted new zeal to my waning efforts, and again renewed my fondest hopes of success. How cheerfully and liberally have I been assisted by his bounty! I had hoped, one day, to have shown him that the advantages I derived there-from are not bestowed in vain. But this hope is now taken from me without having the satisfaction of seeing him in his last moments, to thank and ask Heaven's blessing on him. Death has snatched him from us, and you, with many others, as well as myself, must feel the void that cannot be filled.'

Many testimonials to Mr. Reed's worth outside the artistic circle might be given; but as this is to be shown in another way, I pass them to dwell for a moment on the effect of Mr. Reed's example. One instance has already been stated in the case of the commission given by Mr. Samuel Ward to Mr. Cole for the 'Voyage of Life,' stimulated by the success of the 'Course of Empire.' More striking evidence of it appears in the following facts. Two years after Mr. Reed's death, the exhibitions of the National Academy of Design displayed nearly double the number of works contributed by nearly twice the number of artists that are found in those of the two previous years. In ten years, private collections containing American works alone were rapidly formed and continued to increase, among which those of Mr. Jonathan Sturges, Mr. A. M. Cozzens, Mr. C. M. Leupp, Mr. Thomas H. Faile, Mr. R. M. Oliphant, Mr. Marshall O. Roberts, and others, members of the Sketch Club, or business associates of Mr. Reed, are most conspicuous. Lastly, many

institutions had sprung up in New York, where available capital
for art and a liberal public spirit had immensely increased and
given the city an artistic reputation throughout the country.
Most conspicuous is the 'American Art Union,' founded in
1840, whose subscribers were obtained in all parts of the Union,
and which distributes broadcast among them hundreds of works
by native artists, together with large original engravings illustrative of local life and history, and which could not otherwise
have been published.   At length, in honour of Mr. Reed, the
'New York Gallery of Fine Arts' came into being.   This
institution, the history of which is briefly narrated below, arose
not only in commemoration of him and his services in the cause
of native art, but was intended to be the nucleus of a free public
museum for the city of New York.   Before entering on the
details of its short career, it is sufficient to state, with regard
to Luman Reed and the beneficent effect of his example, that
in his time and generation he made native art the fashion.
Except in the encouragement of local art on a grander scale,
it may be observed that no European potentate, possessing the
will and the power to foster art, surpassed him in spirit or in
act ; the superiority of papal or royal amateurs consisted wholly
in superior resources.   In conclusion, I quote an anonymous
appreciation of Mr. Reed, taken from a newspaper the year of
his death :—

   'It is well to tell the young artist who has to make his way
in this country that his art once had a generous friend who
sought to advance its interests by considering the feelings and
capacities of its votaries. This was encouragement of the right
stamp. To call Mr. Reed a patron of art in the usual acceptation
of the word is to give a feeble idea of his usefulness and of the

spirit which animated him. He aimed to smooth the path of art for those who travelled it by letting them pursue it as was most agreeable to themselves. If he ever sought to point the way by making suggestions or requesting favours, it was done with that consideration for the artist's inclinations which made it gratifying to oblige him. It was not alone this motive, however, which prompted an acquiescence with his views. Though not possessing an educated judgment, he had a natural pictorial perception and good taste which were almost always in sympathy with the more extended knowledge of his artistic friends. A gentleman observing his munificence once remarked to him, " These pictures, Mr. Reed, must have cost considerable money." " They did," he replied ; " the outlay is my pleasure —I like it; besides," his eye lighting up as he spoke, " the artists are my friends, and it is the means of encouragement and support to better men than myself." '

The testimonial in honour of Luman Reed, intended to show the estimate of him by his contemporaries—unfortunately not successful—is the establishment of the New York Gallery of Fine Arts. Four years after his death, it became necessary to close his estate and dispose of his art treasures: the idea occurred to his friends and beneficiaries to secure their purchase by a subscription among Mr. Reed's business associates who, recognising his superior ability as a merchant, would be glad to honour his character and career in this way. This idea was matured and carried out. A subscription was opened, and thirteen thousand dollars, the amount required for the purpose, was immediately obtained. Mr. Theodore Allen, son-in-law of Mr. Reed, in concurrence with others, devised the plan of the institution ; Mr. Jonathan Sturges, Mr. Reed's partner, was made

president of it, which function involved the contribution of most
of the preparatory funds necessary for its establishment ; Mr.
Thomas H. Faile, who contributed the rest, was made treasurer.
Fifty trustees, mostly wholesale grocers, along with other prominent merchants, constituted nominally a board of control—
which rarely met—while the fundamental idea for the maintenance of the institution, as far as revenue was concerned,
consisted of a membership, obtainable by anybody on the payment of one dollar for life. It was thought that for such a
trifling sum the people would flock to the exhibition *en masse.*
Ten thousand certificates of membership were made ready for
' the rush.' The next object was to secure the favourable help
of the press, which was easily accomplished. The claims of the
institution to public support, with a programme of its purpose,
and a list of the fifty trustees attached to it, were presented,
among other editors, to Mr. James Gordon Bennett, of the *New
York Herald.* Mr. Bennett read it over, and on doing so,
slowly and gruffly remarked, ' Why, these people know more
about pork and molasses than they do about art !' ' Yes, that
is true, Mr. Bennett,' was the reply, ' but they give the money.'
' Well,' said he, ' I'll notice it,' and he did the following day.
Next came the problem of an exhibition-room. A suitable
building would require a large endowment—which was not to
be thought of. The National Academy of Design, then occupying
the upper stories of the Society Library building on the corner
of Franklin Street and Broadway, loaned its rooms for the first
display of the collection. Finally, it was suggested that it would
be well to apply to the municipal corporation for the ' Rotunda,'
built by Vanderlyn in 1817 at the north-east corner of the park,
on city property, for his exhibition purposes, now unoccupied,

and which might be had, probably, free of rent. At that time Mr. James Harper, lately elected as a reform candidate, was Mayor, and it was feared that he would oppose the application on the score of the impropriety of giving public property for private purposes. His favourable consent, however, was soon obtained. The next difficulty consisted in getting the Common Council to pass a Bill sanctioning the grant. Some bribery was used and a good deal of ' lobbying.' Besides this, speeches had to be made by the aldermen in favour of it. One of these was Mr. Abraham Cozzens, of hotel celebrity; 'posted' on the history of art by his son, Mr. A. M. Cozzens, he became so entangled and confused in his argumentative use of Greek and Renaissance terms and facts as to endanger the success of the Bill had this depended on what he said. The Bill passed, nevertheless, with only one stipulation, that the building should be vacated, on due notice, whenever wanted. As soon as its possession was ensured, repairs and improvements were made, in the shape of a division of the interior into two stories, and the pictures were hung. To add to the interest of the collection, presents and loans were obtained from artists and others. ' The New York Gallery of Fine Arts' accordingly existed. Here were quarters which, if tenable for ever, might have sufficed for the maintenance of the institution. But events did not shape that way. The expected 'rush' of the masses did not take place. One thousand certificates of membership were with difficulty given away or sold ; but never was enough money obtained to pay expenses. In answer to an inquiry one day by one of the trustees, reminded of the existence of the exhibition only by a chance encounter with an official, ' How does that thing get along?' he replied, mournfully, ' Not at all.' Neither

s

members nor officers (except the two above named) cared enough about the institution to attend an election of its officers ; on the last election that took place one vote only was cast. After an unmolested occupancy of the Rotunda for about two years, the Common Council ordered its evacuation and it was given up.   During this period Mr. Sturges and Mr. Faile supplied the deficiencies of income ; the former, satisfied that it was useless to try to maintain an institution of this stamp, then took steps to close it.   Arrangements were made with the New York Historical Society to accept the collection on condition that the rights and privileges of members should be guaranteed.   Thus did the New York Gallery of Fine Arts end its days as an independent institution.   The collection of works of art made by Mr. Reed now reposes in the attic of a building where no ray of sunlight ever reaches the pictures, and where the few who visit it know nothing of the origin and purpose of the collection.

CHAPTER IX.

THE above period of four years, in which my father became a painter, may be called the turning-point of his life. Before this he had been merely groping his way. The advent of Mr. Reed enabled him to discard fears and doubts, for he now felt that he could change his profession without risk. Disappointment and sorrow, due to the loss of Mr. Reed, somewhat checked his course, deprived as he was of encouragement in the line of art he preferred : his taste tended towards figure-painting through previous practice in drawing and designing, and this taste Mr. Reed had fostered. He soon found that there was no one possessing the same comprehensive, liberal, and generous spirit to take his place. Our artist, accordingly, had to rely—as before on engraving—on the natural inspiration of the community and accommodate himself to its taste. Meanwhile he had gained some reputation in portraiture, which would ensure him a livelihood, and likewise as a landscape-painter—a branch of art that now began to obtain a foothold in the community, as we see in the success of Cole. He was not discouraged ; on the contrary, he laid down the graver and took up the brush with renewed ardour—not that of an inexperienced and reckless youth, but of a self-reliant man in the prime of life and fully aware of the risks he was to encounter.

Sufficient notice has been taken of the figure-subjects executed by the artist up to this period. Purely tentative before Mr. Reed came on the stage, those which were painted for him only can be considered as professional work. The following subjects, executed afterwards to please himself, complete the list. In 1837 he painted two pictures that have since been destroyed in accordance with his desire : one a 'Ruth and Naomi,' begun in Florence, and the other 'Healing the Possessed,' painted after his return from Europe, the latter an ambitious composition representing Christ casting out devils, in which the principal figure is the maniac at the feet of the Saviour. These may be called his last attempts at 'high art.' In 1838 he painted for Mr. Ogden Haggerty 'Rip van Winkle introduced to the crew of Hendrick Hudson in the Catskill Mountains '— a ghostly assembly playing ninepins in a low, weird, supernatural light, the effect of which, together with the humour of the scene, were adequately rendered. One of my father's favourite ideas had been the possibility of combining figures and landscape together so as to make each equally interesting, and not, as usual, depicting the latter as a mere background to the former. One case of this kind has already been mentioned, the figures, however, being portraits. Another instance is 'A Dance on the Battery in presence of Peter Stuyvesant,' painted for Mr. Thomas Hall Faile. In spite of certain technical defects, the grouping and action of the youthful dancers, the out-door effect, the gaiety of the scene, and the benevolent expression of the old governor, express the spirit of the subject. The last of his perform-

LAST INTERVIEW BETWEEN WASHINGTON AND HARVEY BIRCH.

' "Does your Excellency think that I have exposed my life and blasted my character for money? ... Not a dollar of your gold will I touch." The bag fell at the feet of the pedler.

' "Remember your risks and cares. I have told you that the characters of men who are much esteemed in life depend on your secrecy; what pledge can I give them of your fidelity?"

' "Tell them," said Birch, advancing and unconsciously resting one foot on the bag, "tell them that I would not take the gold." ' — *The Spy*, by J. Fenimore Cooper.

Reproduced from the Original Picture in the possession of Miss Fanny Gilliss, Washington, D.C. Heliogravure Dujardin. Printed by C. Wittmann.

ances in this direction, painted some years afterwards, will be mentioned later on. His most successful attempt in historical art was a small picture entitled ' Last Interview between Harvey Birch and Washington,' exhibited in 1843 and engraved for one of the Annuals. This was a picture for which he was able to secure models ; its success indicates a certain proficiency and excites regret that he was obliged to abandon historical art. Bought by the American Art Union, it fell into the hands of the Hon. George P. Marsh. It is well to note in this connexion that the literature and art of the new country went hand in hand.

The dominance of portraiture in the art of the day, and the reason for it, has already been dwelt on. The lover of a portrait is the type of the local patron of art. Few picture-buyers at that time ever got beyond that point. As the exhibitions of the National Academy of Design annually presented the artistic harvest of the season, and as the majority of works exhibited were portraits, this fact denotes the natural taste of the public. The exhibitions were, of course, extremely monotonous. The complaint was often heard, ' Why don't artists paint something else ? ' Nevertheless, portraiture brought the friends of its subjects to the exhibition, and, consequently, a crowd which put money into the purse of the National Academy of Design. Many of these portraits possessed great merit. Those of ladies by Ingham, remarkable for feminine refinement, always secured marked attention. The portraits of Inman, as well as those by Sully, Morse, and Page, met with the same favour. Development in other branches of art kept pace, in a measure, with portraiture. Landscapes increased in number, and occasionally a picture in the exhibition by a

foreign artist added to the variety of attractive art. In the
way of local landscapes, there were the works of Hoyle,
Doughty, and especially Cole. Add to these the contributions in figure-subjects of Weir, Chapman, and Mount, with
those of Inman. The school of American art was now fully
established. Soon a new generation of artists sprang up, and
the exhibitions became more complete and popular. No pictures
were refused ; on the contrary, the town was ransacked for
them. Anybody that could daub a canvas with colour and
produce any sort of pictorial effect was deemed an artist,
and his productions were welcome. The Press, it must be
noted, now began to entertain the public with art, not editorially
or by criticism, but in the way of complaints by anonymous
correspondents. In the spring of 1838 our artist, who had
the misfortune to be on the 'Hanging Committee' of the
Academy, became the subject of newspaper attack, as narrated
in the following letter to Mr. Cole :—

'Since you left here the current of things has not brought
much within my view of an agreeable character that has not
been more than overbalanced by its opposite ; still, I am
plodding on in spite of wind or weather, urged on by the
charmer, Hope, "whatever ills betide." I am the chief scape-
goat of the notorious hanging committee of the Academy, or,
rather, I am believed, myself alone, to be that multitudinous
animal, the Council, with seven heads and ten horns, if one
may judge by an article in the *Standard*. Our long-cherished
institution has imbibed the disorganizing contagion that has
so long prevailed in the political community ; its hitherto
healthy growth is impeded, I fear, for ever. Every day dis-
closes some additional subject of complaint ; the most un-

charitable construction is put on the conduct of the Council, and, without witness or jury, the *soi-disant* judges of the day pronounce awful sentences of condemnation — " Partiality," " favouritism," " keeping down young artists," " hoisting up Academicians;" " Why are such vile daubs placed on the line and such artistic productions left to blush unseen in the shade ? " The secret of all this is the influx of mediocre talent and the hot-bed fermentation visible among juvenal* artists to ripen before their time, and by unnatural means generated by the ill-judged zeal of interested friends or unenlightened admirers.'

But such are the common experiences of people who work for the public. In the same letter he adds, ' The times are dull.' No Mr. Reed existed to stimulate him ; nevertheless, the impulse he gave to art was still operative, and my father still had sufficient employment. Among the lovers of art of the day, and a special friend, Mr. Jonathan Sturges, partner of Mr. Reed and the inheritor of his artistic purposes, was the most conspicuous. Besides executing portraits and land-scapes for his collection, my father owed him advantages which will be stated further on. Another prominent aid was Mr. Frederick J. Betts, living at Newburgh, where adjoining his house he had built a gallery for paintings. My father executed for this gentleman several portraits, a landscape called ' Saturday Afternoon,' and two others, ' Morning and Evening of Life,' of larger dimensions than usual and exhibited in 1840. Other works of the same character were painted and disposed of. ' Western Emigrants ' and ' The Rainbow,' purchased by two amateurs of Cincinnati ; ' The Stranded Ship,' painted for Mr. James Brown of New York ; a ' Sailing Party,' and others,

---

* ' Most brisky juvenal.'—*Midsummer Night's Dream*, Act 3, Sc. 1.

which found sympathetic appreciators. All these works belong
to the ideal class, in which the artist's brush is free. In
addition to these he painted two 'portrait-landscapes,' which
indicate the sort of art patronage that springs out of personal
associations, and which illustrate the kind of public taste a
painter must sometimes gratify. The following extract from a
letter of a certain ' patron ' shows its character :—

'My brother is determined that you shall paint a picture for him of
this village. The point from which the picture is to be taken is about
one mile west. I have been there to-day with my friend Mrs. ——,
and we have settled that the subject is without doubt the finest in
creation, to say nothing of the additional interest of its being our native
place.'

The other 'portrait-landscape' was commissioned by Mr.
Ithiel Town, an architect and possessor of a library, who
stipulated that my father should accept pay for it in rare old
books The same person likewise ordered a characteristic landscape of Cole on the same terms. My father was to paint a
view of ' Athens in Greece,' according to a restoration of the
ancient city as depicted in a well-known engraving, which was
to be pasted on a canvas and serve as the drawing of the
subject. All that he had to do that could be called original
was to add colour and atmospheric effect. It is sufficient to
state that he accomplished the task to the satisfaction of the
party concerned, and that, in the course of time, the painting
fell into the hands of a picture-dealer and was consumed in a
conflagration of his premises.

The following extract, from a letter by Mr. Cole, shows the
character and fate of the commission he was favoured with :—

'Do you know I have received a letter from Mr. Town, telling me that neither he nor his friends like the picture I have painted for him, desiring [expecting] me to paint another in place of it, composed of rich and various landscape, history, and architecture of different styles and ages—these are his own words—ancient or modern Athens. This letter is interlarded with fulsome panegyrics on my excellence in such pictures : " My friend Cole is celebrated for painting rich landscapes and architecture, history, &c., intermixed." You and I painting modern and ancient Athens with the aid of prints, " full of poetry or reality, and full of the most intense interest to everybody of literary character who should behold them "—and full of trumpery if they resembled this twaddle. For this trashy stuff—after I have painted him a picture as near as I could accommodate my pictorial ideas to his prosaic voluminousness—a picture of immense labour, at a much lower price than I have painted pictures of the same amount of labour for several years past—he expects me again to spend weeks and weeks after the uncertain shadow of his appreciation ! I will not do it, and I have written to him to say that I would rather give back his books and consider the commission as null than [repeat] it on such precarious terms. The picture was painted for him and is his. . . . On this subject I will say no more, but beware when you paint for the same patron.'

Another example of this sort of taste is pertinent. One day a genteel old lady with a bundle of engravings under her arm called upon my father, and introduced herself by stating that she wished to engage him to paint a landscape for her. She had always admired his trees, and wanted a picture composed mainly of these objects. Unrolling her engravings she pointed to a group in one of them which pleased her very much, also another group in another engraving which was to be copied and placed in front of that group. In one corner of the picture a thicket was to be introduced, from which a lion was to be seen rushing towards a river with a lamb on the shore. The sky was not to occupy much space; the rest of the canvas should be filled with trees. She had made a

T

tracing of a stump which she greatly admired, and this was to
appear somewhere in the foreground.   The river was to be
called the Jordan, and John the Baptist with the Saviour were
to be seen standing up to their knees in the water.   On my
father remarking that these models, copied indiscriminately from
works by Rubens, Poussin, Claude, and other modern painters,
were not consistent with Oriental history, she replied that 'any
other baptism would do as well.'   Finally, on his declining the
commission, she regretted this very much, as she had been
reflecting on the design for two years, and had brought the
material with her to save the artist trouble.

Another would-be patron of art, one of the notabilities
of the time, must not be overlooked.   The following letter,
accompanied by a prospectus, of which extracts are given
below,* explains itself:—

'BARNUM'S AMERICAN MUSEUM,
'NEW YORK, *June* 21, 1855.
'A. B. DURAND, ESQ.
'DEAR SIR,—At the proper time I should like you to paint
one or more of the Premium Portraits for the Gallery of Beauty, and

---

* 'An eminent publishing house in Paris is engaged in issuing a series of
the most distinguished FEMALE BEAUTIES in the world, which, when completed,
is to include TEN of the most beautiful ladies in the United States and the
Canadas.   In order to obtain such specimens of American beauty as will
compare favourably with any that the Old World can produce, as well, also,
as to secure in a permanent form a Gallery of Original Portraits, unequalled in
the world for graceful perfection, and at the same time encourage a more
popular taste for the Fine Arts, stimulate to extra exertion the genius of our
Painters, and laudably gratify the public curiosity, the subscriber will give
over FIVE THOUSAND DOLLARS IN PREMIUMS.   To accomplish these objects, he
proposes that every person having a fair friend (single or married) whom he
believes competent to compete for the premiums and *éclat* embraced in this
enterprise, shall forward to him (free of expense) her photograph or daguerreo-

will thank you to write me immediately, in confidence, naming your lowest terms.

'As the premiums will necessarily be a source of inordinate expense to me, I hope you will be as considerate as you can in the price demanded.

'It is, perhaps, unnecessary for me to mention that the exhibition of these portraits will afford an excellent opportunity to enhance your already well-earned popularity, as each portrait will bear the name of its distinguished artist.

'Truly yours,

'P. T. BARNUM.'

One of my father's inferior works, picked up at auction, chanced to find its way into a private collection, where, in comparison to other works, it did him great injustice. He accordingly addressed a note to the owner of it, offering to substitute a superior picture. The following is the reply:—

'. . . . As to the picture, I have always thought better of this

---

type. A sealed envelope must accompany each portrait, enclosing the address (with or without the real name of the fair original), furnishing the colour of her eyes, the shade of her complexion, and a small lock of her hair, in order that the artists may do their celebrity and their subjects justice in executing the subsequent Gallery of Oil Paintings. Of these envelopes, none except those accompanying the one hundred likenesses that receive the PREMIUMS will be opened; and although no lady's name will be exacted as a right, it is hoped that those to whom the Premiums may be awarded, will not ultimately object to allow their real names to be attached to the Oil Portraits, and published in the French *World's Book of Female Beauty*. . . . Every visitor, on entering the gallery devoted to the daguerreotypes, shall receive a slip of paper, upon which he or she may mark down the particular numbers of the *one hundred* (or less) portraits, out of the entire collection, which he or she may conceive best entitled to premiums. As the visitor passes out, this slip shall be taken and deposited in a box at the door, under the close supervision of a special receiver. Each lady who may secure one of the ten highest premiums, will be desired to sit to the best artist in the city nearest to her residence, who will paint her portrait, from life, for the French publication, at the expense of the subscriber.'

specimen than I know you have done. Some day, when I meet with
a first-class, A 1, super-extra, super-interesting and characteristic Durand,
I will lay my sacrilegious paws upon it; but I am hard to suit, for I
require not only fine artistic qualities, but also interest in the subject;
then it must suit me; and then it must work in with my other pictures
and subjects. For these reasons it happens that I generally stumble
accidentally on the pictures I buy, but don't find them when I go to
look for a particular thing. Hoping for success some time,—I remain,
&c.'

Mr. Cole and my father, both labourers in the same professional field, and subject to the same trials and social conditions,
the former living in the charming Catskill region, and the latter
in the uncongenial city, corresponded regularly and sometimes
compared notes. The following extracts from two letters afford
a glimpse of their respective moods, and may interest some of
my readers, especially artists. My father writes:—

'I am still willing to confess myself a trespasser on your
ground, though, I trust, not a poacher; landscape still occupies
my attention. If the public don't wish me to take their heads,
I will, like a free horse, take my own, and "ope the expanding
nostril to the breeze." Now, if there be a man on earth whose
location together with whose locomotive powers I envy, it is
Thomas Cole! I am free to say that, were I so circumstanced,
and still in possession of my present combustibility of nerve and
certain other impetuosities, the seven-league boots of Jack the
Giant-killer would not even be desirable. This miserable little
pen, enclosing 250,000 human animals or more, should no longer
hold me to swell the number; the vast range of this beautiful
creation should be my dwelling-place, the only portion of which
I can at present avail myself being the neighbourhood of
Hoboken, which I am permitted to strip of its trees and

meadows two or three times a week, and for which I am indeed thankful. How do you get on?'

Mr. Cole replies:—

'I am sorry that you are at times so much depressed in spirits. You must come to live in the country. Nature is a sovereign remedy. Your expression is the result of debility; you require the pure air of heaven. You sit (I know you do) in a close, air-tight room, toiling, stagnating, and breeding dissatisfaction at all you do, when if you had the untainted breeze to breathe, your body would be invigorated, your spirits buoyant, and your pictures would even charm yourself. This is not exaggeration—there is much sober truth in it. You speak of the want of proper excitement. I am of the opinion that in the city more excitement is necessary than in the country ; and particularly so to artists like ourselves. In the city we are surrounded by our fellow-men and we feel their presence ; we labour for their approbation, and require that stimulant frequently. But in the country we labour under more healthy influences. The desire to produce excellence feeds the flame of our enthusiasm, and I believe the product is worthier than that which is wrought out to the approbation of the many around us. In the country we have necessarily to defer the reward of the approbation of our fellows, and have time to examine critically our own works and form a judgment of our own that cannot be jostled out by that of every new observer. You will think me sermonising ; but I merely wish to convince you that, provided you could consistently leave the city, you would be better in health and spirits, and I am sure if you would pitch your tent near me, I should also be benefited—so there you see I come in with a little selfishness at last!'

Circumstances were not favourable to my father's removal to the country. On the contrary, a city life, however distasteful to him, became more imperative than ever on account of his profession of a portrait-painter, which obliged him to dwell where his sitters dwelt. For his friend Cole, exclusively a landscape-painter, the country afforded every advantage. Again, early in this period—1834—my father married his second wife, Mary Frank, daughter of Jacob Frank, Esq., which rendered a removal to the country impracticable. Always in quest of picturesque material in summer, and leading a sort of nomadic life for eight years, often separated from his children, and, again, the owner of a house, he was only too glad to return to it, especially as it was now within the city limits. He accordingly took possession of his old home in 1838, where he was to remain for thirty-one years. Two years later he added a studio, and considered himself settled for life.

Europe is the Mecca of an American artist. Every painter and sculptor longs to make this pilgrimage, and, indeed, finds it indispensable for the completion of his education. A writer may develop his mental faculties in libraries containing the literary masterpieces of the greatest intellects of all nations; he can here study their methods and style, comprehend their motives and ideas, and commune with them in their books mind to mind. The artist to commune with the master-minds of his profession must see the works actually executed by them, real and not abstract products of their brain, and learn from them directly; not until he stands in front of the paintings on the walls of the great galleries of Europe and studies the forms and colour which the artists' own hands have placed on the canvas, does he find the libraries that furnish professional knowledge and show him the modes, compass, and depth of artistic thought. The time had now come for the artist to go abroad. Thanks to the facilities afforded him by his friend, Mr. Jonathan Sturges, who relieved him from the financial cares of the journey, he was able to undertake it, and to this we now turn.

CHAPTER X.

Tour in Europe—Steamer Life—George Combe—'Old Masters' in London—
C. R. Leslie—Sir David Wilkie—Appreciation of the English School of
Art — A Masquerade — London and the Country — Switzerland — Italy —
Works executed in Florence—Claude Lorraine—Life in Rome—Voyage
Home—Icebergs—Arrival.

FOUR years had elapsed since, through the advent of
ocean steamers, a voyage to Europe had been rendered
easy, comfortable, and, it may be added, commonplace.
Travellers in foreign lands on returning home were no longer
regarded with awe—now alone accorded to the explorers of the
Dark Continent. People crossed the 'big ferry' with comparatively little risk, were rarely robbed abroad except by hotel-
keepers, kept journals, returned home and resumed their daily
avocations, without becoming, as formerly, when ocean navigation was thought perilous and bandits abounded on the
Continent, either heroes or 'lions.' Some crossed for pleasure,
many for business, and few, as nowadays, for instruction alone.
My father belonged to the latter class. Fortunately he kept a
journal in the style of letters, afterwards transcribed in his
correspondence, and as the experiences and observations therein
recorded reveal character, opinions, and sentiments, I quote
freely from it.

In company with his young artist friends, Messrs. Casilear,
Kensett, and Rossiter, he sailed for London in the steamer
British Queen, June 1, 1840. The journal begins on board

the steamer, 'with a degree of composure of mind quite
unexpected after the painful parting from family and friends.'
A rose given him by his youngest daughter is recorded the
next day as 'still fresh and fragrant;' the day after, 'in full
bloom and as yet unfaded—a good omen that all are well at
home, which may God grant!' and finally, the fourth day out,
'having bloomed its little hour, it has scattered its leaves on the
water.' No longer thus reminded of home associations, he now
turns his attention to the world around him, of which he speaks
in this fashion :—

'Really, at a superficial glance, this vessel appears to be little
else than an immense cookshop and slaughter-house afloat; the
business of eating seems to take precedence of all other. . . . .
The dinner closes with songs and sentiments in the saloon ; on
deck, the merry contagion spreads and continues through the
afternoon, when the evening closes in with dance and song
among the sailors. All is joy and glee.'

The first Sunday out, a Scotch Presbyterian preaches on the
'disobedience of Jonah.' After the sermon, 'Fell into conversation with a Mr. H—— of New York, who, besides possessing
consummate knowledge of painters and pictures, gave me to
understand that he was the only man living who comprehended
Shakespeare.'

Mr. George Combe, the eminent phrenologist and author of
The Constitution of Man, is on board. 'Had some conversation
with Mr. Combe on the moral condition of the people of the
United States. He confirmed the decision of Dr. Spurzheim
that we are, in the aggregate, deficient in conscientiousness and
moral culture, and, consequently, in danger of Government
dissolution, unless an amount of intelligence superior to what

PORTRAIT OF A CHILD.

Engraved by H. Manesse from the Original Picture in the possession of F. F. Durand.

has yet been attained by any other nation shall be diffused among the people. We possess ample means to effect that object when rightly directed, although our present condition exhibits much of discouragement; he by no means despairs of our arriving at that result by the gradual extension of an enlightened system of education, by which means alone permanency to our moral or religious institutions can be secured.

‘It is said that a man-of-war at sea is a perfect despotism in miniature; not so with a steam-packet. On the contrary, it is rather an example of a perfect democracy—for instance, immediately in front, flat on the deck, on a small coiled rope, squatted like a tailor, George Combe, the phrenologist and philosopher; near him, without even a coiled rope or seat of any kind other than the bare deck, two or three fashionable ladies; near them, on a wooden bench, sits an Italian bishop surrounded by several of his *confrères*, consisting of priests and laymen, smoking segars (puffing forth a more harmless fire and smoke than at some other times proceed from the mouths of that description of personage); while all around in almost every possible position—sitting, standing, reclining, or stretched out at full length—appear ladies and gentlemen, soldiers and sailors, officers and crew, men and women of all nations and tongues, all apparently in full possession of equal rights and liberty of conscience.

‘To-day again is Sunday. I do not attend the church service, the better to indulge reflection unrestrained under the high canopy of heaven, amidst the expanse of waters. This mode of passing the Sabbath became habitual with me in early life—then ’midst other scenes than here, it is true; yet if more consonant with my feelings (as the world of woods, plains, and

U

mountains ever is), certainly not less impressive. All the sounds of inanimate nature are of mournful solemnity—the rush of many waters as on the mighty ocean, the roar or whisper of the winds through the shadowy forest, the endless murmur of the waterfall, the patter of the summer shower, all tending to excite mournful meditation.

'Two glorious objects met my view to-day—the first sight of the rising sun and the first sight of land.' Standing by the side of Mr. Combe as the steamer glides by the varied coast of England, the artist remarks, 'It is a beautiful world, Mr. Combe.' 'Yes,' replies the philosopher, 'but what a pity man is not in harmony with it.'

The traveller landed in England, June 17, 1840. Nature now gives way to Art. Another world opens before him. On reaching London his first purpose is to see 'Old Masters.' Other sights and wonders, of course, receive attention, but those of art are paramount. Apart from the professional interest of his observations, his notes are curious in another way: we have the judgment of a self-taught artist, with no teacher or guide but nature, on the works of superior artists who had enjoyed every professional advantage, as well as all the public support that time and social development could furnish. The day after his arrival he goes to the British Institution, containing a fine collection of 'Old Masters' derived from private galleries.

'I repaired there with my companions to enjoy for the first time the long and fervently desired view of genuine works by the Old Masters. I saw them without suspicion of their originality—Wouvermans, Cuyp, and Van de Velde, Rubens, Van Dyck and Murillo, Poussin, Both, Carlo Dolce, the Carracci and Guercino, Teniers, Ostade, and Gerard Dow.' Subsequently, on visiting the National Gallery, he adds, ' I have seen the Old Masters again. With some I am not a little disappointed, and must confess that only a few, if any, surpass my preconceived notions,' and these are Rubens, Murillo, Van Dyck, Rembrandt, Both, Cuyp, and Salvator Rosa. He speaks in qualified terms of Claude, the leading artistic divinity on landscape, and yet ' what I have seen of his works is worth a passage across the Atlantic.'

Next come living English painters and their works, of which the following extracts from the journal convey a general idea.

The Royal Academy Exhibition is soon disposed of. ' Some few pictures are of an elevated character, or, at least, display elements of high intellectual effort, especially in conception and design ; at the same time these are marred by crudities. I observe only in a few works expression and character, while correctness in drawing, solidity, finish—naturalness, in short, I look for in vain.' The exhibition of watercolours, however, excites admiration. ' The higher qualities of these works are by no means inconsiderable. I question whether they do not evince an equal, if not a higher, degree of talent than the oil pictures of the Royal Academy. The sketchy style and artificial management (pervading faults of the English school) appear, if not appropriate, at least less objectionable in water-colour than in oil pictures. One hardly expects the sober, quiet tone, the depth and mellowness, the transparency and glow in the former department, which is found in the finished productions of the latter. I was accordingly agreeably surprised to find these qualities in no small degree among the watercolour productions both in landscape and figure subjects, even to a greater extent than in most of the corresponding productions in oil, also in the higher traits of fine character and expression occasionally met with. Their aim, however, appears too generally directed to the attainment of brilliant and striking effects, both in light and dark as well as in colour. The quiet loveliness of Nature, the subdued and modest aspect, brilliant without crudeness and rich without glare, like the gentle and most estimable virtues of the moral world, are but too often forced down or overlooked amidst the glitter and exuberance of ostentatious display.'

Leaving pictures for painters, he calls on Mr. C. R. Leslie. 'The evening passed in the most agreeable manner, chiefly devoted to looking over a portfolio of sketches in water-colours, produced at several years' meetings of the long-established Sketch Club of which Mr. Leslie is a member. This portfolio contains sketches by A. E. Chalon and brother, Uwins, Stanfield, Landseer, Partridge, Crystall, and Leslie himself. Many were begun and finished in one evening, particularly those of A. E. Chalon, the most conspicuous for gracefulness, composition, and character. . . . All present a surprising display of imagination and graphic skill, especially when it is taken into account that they are extempore works.'

Mr. Leslie having favoured him with an introductory letter to Sir David Wilkie, he visits this artist the next day.

'We were shown into a drawing-room hung with numerous engravings from his own pictures. Sir David soon presented himself—a blunt, honest-looking Scotchman, of rather gruff aspect and manner. After a few brief inquiries relating to our voyage, he conducted us into his *atelier* and there disclosed without reserve the secrets—the very *modus operandi* of his professional labour. He showed us first his picture of

Columbus demonstrating the probability of the existence of another continent to three or four personages on his first visit to Spain, as related by Irving. Figures as large as life and of fine character, and the story is well told ; but a picture of inferior merit compared with his smaller works. Of the latter there were several on his easels, merely commenced ; one in particular, in which there were ten or a dozen heads beautifully laid in and nearly finished ; other parts of the canvas were untouched, except a careless drawing-in of the general design, with small portions of figures and patches of background slightly painted. The subject of this picture is " John Knox administering the Sacrament." There were two or three other works of smaller dimensions, one a " Village School," a beautiful composition and replete with nature in the various attitudes and occupations of the juvenile assembly.

'But what most interested me in the interview with Wilkie was the disclosure of his process in painting. The ground of his canvas is white. After having determined his design in general composition and effect of colour by small sketches, the whole is carefully drawn in without any apparent aim at correctness or precision in detail ; the principal heads are then carefully painted, as above specified in the subject of " John Knox," after which the background and the rest of the picture are thinly dead-coloured, indicating the general disposition of colour, light and dark. This done, he proceeds to make careful finished drawings in black and white chalk on tinted paper, from models, of the most important portions of the figures and groups, whole or in part, according to their prominence in the picture ; and from these drawings he paints, and, if I have not misunderstood him, he finishes such parts without recurrence to nature, except in heads, if even there. Many of these studies I saw scattered about his rooms—heads, arms, hands, legs, and feet, all beautifully drawn. Such is a general outline of his process, especially in small compositions. He said that he preferred to paint in the principal heads on the white canvas and at once, as far as practicable, as he thereby obtained more clearness of colour, sharpness, and solidity, rather than dead-colouring an effect after the manner of some who depend on frequent repetitions.'

Mr. Sheepshanks' collection, next visited, furnishes him with a text for remarks on other works by Leslie as well as by other English masters.

' Two by Leslie are among his best works, and one, at least, a scene from the *Merry Wives of Windsor*, unsurpassed perhaps by anything he has ever done. Falstaff, Anne Page, Slender and Shallow—figures in this picture—are in their best dress, and indeed no artist has represented these characters equal to Leslie. There are several of his works illustrating Shakespeare, all very beautiful; but the most recent ones are more crude and less agreeable in tone, though nowise deficient in character. There are also a number by Turner, Stanfield, Constable, Calcott, and Landseer, one by Wilkie, and several by other artists. In Turner I have not yet been able to discern the high degree of excellence which is conceded to him. He appears to me, indeed, the most factitious and artificial of all the distinguished English artists. I discover in him much of imaginative and poetic power, but that appears developed at too great a sacrifice of truth and propriety. At all events, if Turner is to be judged by the acknowledged standard of excellence presented in the works of the Old Masters, or by nature in the commonly received acceptation of the term, he must be found wanting.*

'Edwin Landseer has merits that no one disputes. His dogs and other animals are indeed exquisite, and some of his finest works are in this collection; for manipulation he is doubtless unequalled. There is great sweetness and classic elegance in the coast scenes of Stanfield, always pleasing and often eminently beautiful; yet there is often too much of opacity in his colour and too much of scenic style in his execution. I saw in this collection one picture by Constable evincing more of simple truth and naturalness than any English landscape I have ever before met with.

'In the evening, paid a second visit to Leslie to make our acknowledgments for his kindness and bid him adieu. He showed us several sketches by his deceased friend Constable in water-colour, pencil, and other styles of drawing, exhibiting great attention to Nature under her changing aspects, all from home scenes and common familiar objects; among others, a port-folio of oil studies from clouds and skies in general, with notes on the backs stating the hour of the day, direction of the wind, and kind of weather. All his sketches were very slight, but indicating much naturalness and beauty of effect. Constable was above the influence of want, and hence not dependent on his art for support; his pictures were not popular in his lifetime.

* During this visit he saw Turner, and visited the house where his paintings were kept. Few were admitted to this den, which was a wilderness of accumulated studies and works in every stage of progress. In after years he thus mentions Turner in 'Letters on Landscape Painting' (see Appendix): 'Turner gathered from the previously unexplored sky alone, transcripts of Nature whose mingled beauty of form and chiaroscuro have immortalised him, for the sole reason that he has therein approached nearer to the representation of the infinity of Nature than all that have gone before him.'

'Mr. Leslie stated to us the following fact—which to the admirer of true art is not much to be lamented—that the distinguished Turner has his house literally filled with his own productions; that even in his cellar are stored away many of his former works which he has not looked at himself for years. This accumulation is owing to his extravagant prices, not being obliged to sell at a moderate rate, having acquired great wealth by his drawings made for engraving, of which he has produced an infinite number.'

Such is an estimate of the works of the leading English artists of the day. Of the English school in general he has a less favourable opinion.

'In the school of British art, technicalities evidently receive the principal attention, not from any deficiency in imaginative power or poetic imagery—for these qualities, together with sentiment and character, often abound—but the language in which they are expressed is either inflated in style or replete with affectations, the choice of subject seldom evincing any loftier aim than commonplace passion and scenes of familiar life. Happy touches in execution or felicitous combinations of colour, peculiar or difficult of attainment, or simply of rare occurrence, without reference to naturalness, or consistent with admitted principles of beauty, are sought for and dwelt on with undue admiration ; unobjectionable and perhaps commendable when properly subordinated to higher qualities, these are too often converted into models for imitation—dangerous models, because they are finally aimed at as an end, instead of a means for the attainment of an ulterior object. Everybody knows that too much attention to the mechanism of style, or to conventional rules for painting, necessarily leads to a subversion of the spiritual and intellectual meaning of art. It is thus with the English school. Artificial beauty may at first sight be highly attractive on account of insinuating smiles and graces, but which on close examination is found to be little else than heartless and unmeaning grimace. To make use of another figure, Mistress Art in England tries to impose on her enamoured admirer a painted cheek instead of the glow of health. The last works of Leslie and Wilkie are almost the only exceptions. . . . . Unfortunately, these distinguished painters in their recent productions demonstrate the danger of contact with error, turning, as they have, from their former chaste and true style to the present superficial and negligent, or rather studiously careless, manner of their contemporaries.'

The journal, besides professional observations, contains sundry descriptions of London and its sights, which are thus summed up :—

'In the evening, having been complimented with a ticket, price one guinea, I attended a masquerade ball. Pursuant to regulations, I provided myself with a black mask, to which my sense of propriety was much indebted, for I should have blushed to " see my natural face in a glass," as one of the motley throng assembled on this occasion in this licensed scene of folly and depravity. There were about two or three hundred characters in the assemblage in various costumes, some of them in good taste, some in bad, and others in no taste ; some were masked without any other disguise, and some without any disguise but that of *decent men and women.* Of the female portion in particular, the less said the better. I saw but one or two women whose countenances seemed at variance with the occasion, and one, more especially, whose soft, pensive eye and graceful brow

x

revealed, indeed, " too much of heaven on earth to last "—of
too fair and delicate texture to sustain for length of years the
blighting influence of sensuality and midnight revel. I soon
left the rooms, with no desire to revisit them.

' I have not seen one half of London, but I have perhaps
seen its fairest side. It seems to me a city of prosperity and
abundance ; richness, variety, and often magnificence strike one
at every step through its principal streets, and it is only through
these great thoroughfares that I have passed. That there are
haunts of poverty and wretchedness equally startling, and
perhaps more extended, I well know, but I have not sought
them ; on the contrary, I have avoided them as unprofitable
spectacles and often unsafe. In the country, as far as I have
been, all is like a vast garden of the richest cultivation. The
houses, though mostly old and picturesque from the wear and
tear of time, are always cleanly and neat, with a real air of
comfort and convenience. But I know this is not the case all
over England. It is not difficult to see that the general means
of living are far more slender and limited than with us. The
eagerness to make a penny apparent among the common people,
and the readiness to take money for the slightest service, even
by persons decent and respectable in appearance, who would
consider themselves insulted in America by the offer of a six-
pence, and who are not only ready to accept it but take care
to let you know that they expect it if you withhold it—these
appearances are too frequent not to convince you, at once, that
John Bull is not so rich and happy a fellow as some signs
indicate ; but he has treated me well for the most part, and I
am not disposed to complain.'

The time had come for departure. After passing seven

weeks in London, he leaves for Paris, July 31st. His sojourn in this great city, still more strange than London, with other features of beauty and interest—'Since I have got into France I feel as if I was in reality transformed to another planet'—is devoted to sight-seeing, including, of course, the public collections of art ; but as he is not in Paris for work, and is in haste to get to Switzerland, and especially Italy, the centre of attraction for an artist in those days, he leaves it at the end of a fortnight. I quote from his journal only the following observations of professional import, taken at random :—'David appears to have sown the first seeds of a corrupt style, for, previous to his time, it appears to me that the French possessed much of the purity and chasteness of the Italian school.' He visits the Luxembourg : 'Our next object was the Salle des Tableaux, or picture-gallery, appropriated solely to the works of modern French artists, of which there are about two hundred specimens, most of them large historical subjects and fine examples of the school in this department, in which, in my judgment, the French artists are far superior to the English. It is true these figures are too often academic and what is termed theatrical, with exaggerated action and expression ; but their finished drawing, anatomical correctness, character, and grandeur of composition, entitle them to an elevated rank as a school of art. . . . Paris is indeed the most gay, the most refined, the most filthy and corrupt of all cities, concentrating in itself all that is attractive and all that is repulsive in every other.'

Passing through Belgium, he arrives in Antwerp at the moment of the inauguration of the statue to Rubens, in honour of whom the whole town is *en fête*. 'We had indeed arrived at a fortunate moment to witness the public regard for the fine arts, and the profound veneration in which the citizens of Antwerp, from the highest to the lowest, hold the distinguished masters to which their country has given birth. Wherever we passed, the streets were thronged with happy faces of every class, age, sex, and condition ; all labour was suspended but that of contributing to the festivities. The sidewalks were hung with festoons of white drapery interspersed with ever-greens, together with tablets bearing the name of the great artist and extending through all the principal streets, while PETER PAUL RUBENS, in large white letters by day and illuminated by night, appeared on the spire of the great cathedral, five hundred feet above the ground. It is here that masters in the fine arts are duly honoured ! It makes me proud to be one of the fraternity ! The religious festival of the Virgin, the patroness of Antwerp, was also celebrated in connexion with the *fête* to Rubens, but the Father of the Flemish school of art seemed to have supplanted even the Virgin Mary on this occasion.'

Italy was the objective point of the painter as far as art is concerned; Switzerland seemed the country *par excellence* with respect to nature. Passing through Holland and up the Rhine, both of which excite unbounded admiration, he reaches Basle September 9th, and gives a month to Swiss landscape, which he thus sums up :—

'I had seen pictures of the snow-capped Alps, but I had never seen anything either in pictures or in nature so glorious and beautiful as the real mountains of this unrivalled country. It is in vain to attempt to describe or paint them; their pure white peaks—shining on the clear blue sky or mingling with the light fleecy clouds that seem to love to linger round their summits, in contrast with the soft blue tint of their lower portions, opposed to the rich green hills, luxuriant trees, brown cottages and cultivated fields, the latter traversed with streams or on the borders of the lakes, and these again varied by bold projecting rocks on their shores and by sloping meadows — present that which is most grand and beautiful in creation, all combining the features of spring, summer and winter in one brief view, and in one short day.'

Here the journal ends, October 11th, and is not resumed again with the same attempt at description. The details of the rest of the tour are jotted down in hasty notes. His pilgrimage, of which Rome is the Mecca, finally ends in Italy. On reaching the promised land he lingers awhile on the beautiful Italian lakes, and then passes on to Milan, Venice, Bologna, devoting a few days to each, and at last rests for twenty days in Florence, where he finds his countryman, Horatio Greenough, who makes his sojourn there extremely agreeable. After accomplishing something in the way of painting, he reaches Rome and there settles for the winter. In Florence, unable to copy certain pictures which happen to be engaged by other artists, he begins the ' Ruth and Naomi,' previously mentioned, with which he soon becomes discouraged and sets aside; finding a ' Turk ' in picturesque costume, a vendor of Oriental curiosities and willing to sit for his portrait, he paints him and pleases himself ' better than usual '—doubtless because nature was his model. He next paints a small semi-ideal landscape in which he introduces the Duomo, inspired by a Claude effect. After this he copies Rembrandt's portrait of himself in the Palazzo Vecchio. In one day he ' advanced the head so far as to surprise a young lady who had been employed for weeks on a picture of some female saint, while an English artist told me that my rapidity astonished the Italians.' The effect of the art of Florence on his mind is found in a phrase of one of his letters from that city : 'Could I have passed a few earlier years in Florence I might have been a painter—but not of landscapes!'

It is evident that my father had 'Claude on the brain,' and was puzzled how to estimate the works of the creator—or, at least, populariser—of modern landscape art. Accustomed to regard Claude as a divinity, he found himself in the attitude of a disputer for the truth in relation to a recognised orthodox authority. There seems to have been a struggle in his mind as to which was right, nature or this 'old master.' The following draft of a letter to his friend Mr. Cole, the only one to whom he could express professional doubts, shows the dilemma and his final conclusion in the matter :—

'I am in Florence, as you perceive. You have been here and know what it is much better than I do. I only wish you were here that I might talk to you, and hear from you, at least, something that would assure me that in crossing the Atlantic, the English Channel, the Seine, the Rhine, the Rhone, the Reuss, the Aar, the Po, and finally the Arno, that I have not also crossed the Styx, for I am often sufficiently bewildered, wretched, and desolate to warrant that conclusion. I presume Florence is much the same as when you were here, abounding in the treasures of art and many other objects of exceeding interest and beauty, together with no small degree of filthiness and excessive bell-ringing. How I came here you have yet to learn. I wish I could tell you how I have tugged and toiled up hill and down, over waters, plains, and mountains, thro' towns and cities, palaces and galleries, till my limbs have failed thro' weariness, and my brain (I wish it was larger) has become bewildered. Every desire for novelty and excitement is gratified to satiety. I have gone, like a child on a holiday festival, to look at great personages and their works, and after seeing them I have said to myself, like that awe-stricken individual on seeing Washington, " He is only a man." The old masters were only men, but they were great men, and, like all great men, sometimes did little things, or, at least, things that might be done by little men; and, even in all their greatness, how much was owing to the circumstances of the times and which, under similar circumstances, might not be done in our own day! Still, I would not have you infer that I underrate their greatness, or that I have not enjoyed the privilege of contemplating their works; on the contrary, I have stood before them with the full measure of veneration, and yielded my humble tribute of admiration and applause.

'I presume you would like to know my impression on examining productions which, as poor old Paff used to say, " make boys of us all." In these degenerate times I hear you ask me what I think of them, and of Claude in particular. Well, the first picture that I saw of his disappointed me ; the second, third, fourth—aye, and seventh—did not meet my expectations. All, strictly speaking, were landscapes ; but when I came to his seaports, the " Embarkation of St. Ursula " and the " Queen of Sheba," I could realise his greatness in the glowing atmosphere and moving water. I have also seen others of his landscapes which, in light, colour, truth, and nature in certain points, are worthy of his high reputation. But the result of my observations thus far is the conviction that the glorious field of landscape-painting has never yet been

so successfully, so fully cultivated, not even by Claude, as have
other branches of art depicting the action and passions of men.
The loftiness and pureness of Raphael and others, who have
best succeeded in embodying the immortal spirit of man, leave
little to desire.   Individual objects have perhaps been as well
expressed as paint and skill can ever express them ; and it
may be hopeless to expect more perfect light and atmosphere
than we find in the seaports and, occasionally, other scenes
by Claude.   Still, I have not felt in contemplating them that
I was so completely in the presence of Nature, so absorbed
by her loveliness and majesty, as not to feel that the portrait
of her might be at least, in some important feature, more
expressive of character.   But one result I found in all, as
well in landscape as in figures : those which approach nearest
to the desired perfection bear indisputable marks of deep,
unceasing study and proportionate toil.   In the latter, Paul
Veronese and Rubens appear to me to have accomplished
more with less labour than any others ; but, may it not be—
and in the best works I am convinced it is—that appearances
of ease are but appearances which conceal the real extent of
labour?   You may remember a Claude in the Palazzo Vecchio,
a seaport painted for the Medici family — a glorious work,
but what minute and elaborate finish and what a multitude of
small parts admirably managed and forming a harmonious
whole! So far as I have seen, he attempted nothing beyond
a soft, unruffled day—no storm effect, not even a common
shower.   He has little imagination.   I should suppose his
pictures to be all compositions from nature, often beautiful
and judiciously arranged, yet not remarkable for varied and
picturesque scenery.   His poetry seldom rises above the pastoral

and descriptive; but here he is, indeed, exquisite. He seems to have had no knowledge of English effects, not even of cloud shadows; he is simple and true to Nature in her broad, open light, either of morning or evening, and there finding sufficient charm.'

We now bid good-bye to Claude, and accompany his critic and admirer to Rome. At this time Rome was the art centre of the world. Statues by the great sculptors of antiquity, along with paintings by the equally great artists of the Renaissance epoch, formed the school to which students of art flocked from all countries. Technical secrets were supposed to be got at by copying venerated masterpieces, as if the feeling of genius could be evoked by imitating forms in colour or in marble with the stroke of a brush or the blow of a chisel. Few artists, if any, tried to comprehend the motives of classic or Renaissance art by a study of the sentiments and energies which animated society in these two culminating periods of human grandeur; technical means were not regarded as subordinate, just as style is subordinate to sense in the works of the giants of literature. Winckelman and Lessing, again, the most celebrated art theorists of the day in treating antique art—the former according to alleged æsthetic rules, reducing beauty and expression to mathematical precision, and the latter assigning to art limited emotional impulses—misdirected most minds. Worship of the old masters, nevertheless, was on the wane. The works and powers of French artists in selecting and treating modern subjects, the productions of Gros, Géricault, Vernet, Delaroche, and Delacroix, for example, along with the growing schools of landscapists in France and England, who derived their inspiration direct from nature, and opened up a new field for public

Y

taste, gradually displaced them.   German theories and Italian methods slowly give way to the delineation of events and personages belonging to the actual modern world, at once comprehensible to artists and the public.   The standard of merit, found in the real of the present, instead of the ideals of the past, is established by the schools of Paris, Dusseldorf, and Munich.   Rome, nevertheless, at this period was an attractive city, a place of repose.   Neither politics nor business formed general subjects of conversation, and no newspapers of any account disturbed the mind.   Papal sovereignty suited the temper and interests of the population.   Taxes were adapted to the condition of the poor, and based on the natural activity and resources of the country.   Foreigners half supported a people whose country, like Switzerland, surpasses others in beauty.   Living is cheap.   'I pay eight dollars a month for my studio,' says our artist in one of his letters, which he thinks is dear, 'including two small rooms besides, and six dollars per month for a bedroom at another place, very neat and well furnished.   I pay about seven cents for breakfast, which consists of tea or coffee, half milk, and a couple of rolls. I dine at half-past four on two or three dishes, as may be, good beefsteaks, pudding, &c., which commonly cost about two cents each; then I generally lunch at noon for three or four cents more.'   American artists enjoy other advantages.   Commercial men from America, exhausted by a business life and travelling for health, and who had never bought a work of art, stop at Rome, catch the art infection, and give commissions for pictures and statues which never would have been given at home, to say nothing of the 'original' old masters they buy 'at a bargain' at the suggestion of a courier or hotel-keeper,

Take it altogether, Rome, at this time, unlike the Rome of to-day, with its triple alliance, boulevards, tramways, locomotives, and other 'modern improvements,' afforded an agreeable, tranquil, and picturesque retreat. Our artist enjoyed and profited by it. His intention was to have made numerous copies for which he had commissions, but, unable to get access to the pictures he wanted to copy, he improved his time in another way: governed by his instincts as usual, he painted from nature. What he accomplished is partially recorded in the following extract from one of his letters :—

'I have just commenced a copy of a portrait by Titian for my own study, which I shall finish with three or four days' work, and, when done, if nothing else comes in my way, I shall paint "on my own hook." I am making arrangements for doing some studies from the old "codgers" who walk the streets here in all the dignity of bearded majesty, old patriarchs who go about looking as if they belonged to a period two thousand years ago.'

These old 'codgers,' the models for artists of saints and apostles, with every variety of expression—meek, devout, and energetic, according to the required character of this or that picture—and others again of modern significance, such as the model for bandits, the representative type of Italian human nature adapted to the romantic tastes of travellers, posed to him, eight in number, and, as portraiture, form some of the best of my father's work. Besides these he painted a 'Piper,' one or two peasant women in old-time costumes of the country, and a donkey, which, to give sittings, was hauled up the stone steps of his studio by ropes. The last and most elaborate of his productions in Rome consists of a study from a female model called by him ' Il Pappagallo,' an effort to treat a subject in the tone of an ' old master.'

While thus engaged, his friend, Mr. F. W. Edmonds, arrived, and gave new zest both to his studies and his travels. Mr. Edmonds worked with him in his studio. After finishing their labours, an excursion to Naples and its environs was projected and carried out, occupying about a month. My father, it must be noted, was not fond of travel; its business details worried him, and, moreover, a journey for pleasure took time which he would rather devote to work. The whole tour, indeed, he regards as an exile, and to be got through with as soon as possible. In his journal he often records depression of spirits and longings for home. But the company of a congenial companion revived his energies and made travel less irksome. Time, in any event, was never lost. A multitude of pencil drawings in outline, taken at every place visited by him, attest his industry. With Rome, however, his pilgrimage ended, and he was now to turn his face homeward. In company with Mr. Edmonds he revisited Florence, stopping at various picturesque towns on the way, and next Bologna, Ferrara, Venice, and Milan, reaching Paris the middle of May. On June 20th, 1841, we find him at Liverpool on the deck of the steamer *Britannia*, bound for New York. The following extract from a letter, although written in Switzerland some months previous, expresses the sentiment of the time and occasion :—

' I wish to continue in Europe as long as it shall be pleasant, for the benefits it will yield me as a landscape-painter—for that object no country in the world can equal it ! But for purposes more important, of higher interest than can be found in this or

AN ICEBERG.

Reproduced from the Original Sketch made on the Steamer 'Britannia,' June 1840, in the possession of J. Durand. Heliogravure Dujardin. Printed by C. Wittmann.

any other country, give me our own dear native land! I can look with admiration and wonder on the beauty and sublimity of the scenes now before me ; I can look with gratification and advantage on the great works of art, as I have done in England and on the Continent, and still expect to do in Italy : yet when all this looking and studying and admiring shall have an end, I am free to confess that I shall enjoy a sight of the signboards in the streets of New York more than all the pictures in Europe ; and for real and unalloyed enjoyment of scenery, the rocks, trees, and green meadows of Hoboken will have a charm that all Switzerland cannot boast ; only let me see them in the presence of family and friends, and they in health and prosperity. " Fly swift around, ye wheels of time, and bring the welcome day." '

On the voyage his brush is brought into requisition by a sight of icebergs, of which he makes some water-colour drawings for himself and his fellow - passengers. On reaching Boston, having a few hours of leisure, he visits the Athenæum, where there is an exhibition ' of some old acquaintances which did not look as well as formerly—Stuart is an exception,' the last entry in his journal, and significant in relation to the effect of his tour. One effect of it is apparent in a list of the works executed the first two years after his return, as follows : ' Castle Blonnai,' ' Cottage on Lake Thun,' ' Oberbasle,' and ' View on the Susten Pass,' in Switzerland ; ' Church at Stratford-on-Avon,' in England ; ' Oberwesel,' on the Rhine ; and ' On the Island of Capri,' in the Bay of Naples. All were painted from pencil drawings inscribed with memoranda of colour and clouds ; none were painted direct from nature, and accordingly lack certain essentials of truth and fidelity. In treatment and colour the

Swiss subjects suggest reminiscences of ' old masters,' while the others are painted in conformity with the sentiment of American nature, so different from that of Europe.   In England, with its moist, vapoury atmosphere, mostly a grazing country, where hedges and single trees abound, the foliage of which is richer in hue and their forms more picturesque, the prevailing green is deeper in tone ; on the Continent, with landscape elements unknown in America, a broad expanse of surface not marred by fences, diversified by grey towns and by clusters of red-roofed houses in the villages scattered around, checkered with fields of grain and vines, and where the hills and mountains consist of tinted rocks and crags, the colour is still further removed from green and far richer.   In our ' green forest land,' on the contrary, such elements are wanting.   Our soil, over-spread with an almost uniform culture, consisting of cultivated clearings amidst masses of woods reaching to the tops of all elevations, monotonous and paler in hue on account of the drier climate, is peculiarly green, except late in the autumn, when the dying foliage puts on brilliant tints and colours that transcend the resources of the palette.   In reply to a criticism once made on his works that they were ' too green,' an objection made only after the appearance among us of modern European landscapes, my father simply observed, ' I paint green because I see nature green.'   And so he continued to paint, using other pigments only as the local colours and tints of objects demanded, never forcing his brush according to a conventional theory of colour or the practice of other schools.

CHAPTER XI.

The Period of Production—Prosperity of the Country—The Art Union War—Benefit of the Institution—Record of Works—Resigns the Presidency of the National Academy of Design—Summer Excursions—Life in the Woods — Art in a Western City— Studies from Nature — The *Crayon*— Rise and Decline of the American School.

THE experimental period of my father's painting career having come to an end — that in which he was acquiring knowledge and self-reliance, the productive period—that of the full maturity of his powers—now begins. Portraiture is still his main dependence. A growing dislike of this branch of art, however, owing to the necessity of depicting uninteresting subjects, coupled with the caprices of sitters, especially ladies, determined him to abandon it as soon as possible. Fortunately, his increasing reputation as a landscape-painter enables him to do it safely. Nature now gives him sittings according to his fancy, and finds no fault when he fails to detect and depict her beauty.

Moreover, he can better rely on the support of the community. The times are propitious. Public taste and wealth have increased proportionately. Between 1836 and 1839, in the short period of three years, the prosperity of the country, due to various causes, had increased enormously. The development of the South and West had acquired immense impetus by which New York, the great entrepôt of the continent for both inland and foreign commerce, benefited beyond calculation. Immigration, with its coincident impulses, gave rise to every sort of enterprise, especially land speculation, and to such an extent as soon to bring on a collapse—over-trading, over-production, hard times, and a commercial crisis. In consequence of this, about 1840, universal depression ensued. Society seemed paralysed. Dull times, like a plague, provoked gloomy retrospection. People refrained from amusements. The curtain of the old Park Theatre rose often to audiences of only thirty people ; on one occasion, only one person being present, to whom his money was refunded, the curtain remained down. Public entertainments consisted chiefly of courses of lectures, while revivals, of which Elder Knapp and the Rev. Mr. Kirk were the principal and effective leaders, met with great success. Notwithstanding all this, capital had accumulated, certain fortunes had been secured, incomes were not only liberally but extravagantly expended, and society, as usual, interested itself in other things. Among these, art obtained its share of attention. Art opened another road to new men ambitious of social distinction, and 'many there were who travelled that way.' The American Art Union arose—an institution successfully managed by commercial men ; a fresh, opportune, and powerful patron of art, it exercised an important influence on the development of the American school. Mention of it here is again necessary on account of an incident that reveals a trait of character in the artist as well as in the relationship of this institution to the National Academy of Design.

The rise and fall of the American Art Union is somewhat singular. Starting in 1840 under the title of ' The Apollo Association,' on the lottery principle, it distributed among its members, who became such by a subscription of five dollars, original paintings and engravings by native artists, the latter held to be worth the price of subscription, and given to all members alike. At first the institution ' dragged its slow length along ; ' subsequently, on changing its name to ' The American Art Union,' and conducted by energetic merchants, it flourished. ' The Art Union, in the management of its business, purchased its stock, advertised and exhibited its goods, employed its agents and clerks, just like a merchant.'* One of its prizes, ' The Voyage of Life,' a series of landscape compositions by Cole on four large canvases, offered a temptation so irresistible as to run its subscribers up from eight hundred to sixteen thousand. The progress of the institution, consequently, for a few years was rapid, and to the detriment of the National Academy of Design. Always mistrustful of the injury, the Academy, nevertheless, favoured the growth of its rival in consideration of its benefit to art. ' It would be a happy thing for the world,' says the President of the Academy, quoting a passage from Aristotle, ' if artists were to be made the sole judges of the arts ; but we are favoured with canonists and nobility as arbitrators who are quite unacquainted with our concerns, and these again have certain managers, as they are termed on the stage, or, as Æschines calls them, *pettifoggers of the forum*, who cajole the public.' He endorses the rival institution (then the Apollo Association) in the following terms : ' We do not believe that the class of those who wish to " cajole the public " in this matter is very large ; indeed, we are quite sure that the mass of those who associate for the encouragement of art in our city are impelled by motives truly liberal.' This was un- doubtedly true, and while Mr. Bryant held the office of Presi- dent of the institution, the Academy ran no risk ; but under

* *Art Union Bulletin*, 1853.

his successor, Mr. Prosper M. Wetmore, the spirit of its management changed. An unprecedented income enabled more prizes to be offered than usual, while artists naturally sent their works to the best market, the effect of which was to decrease at once the attraction and the revenue of the Academy exhibitions. In the spring of 1848 the breach between the two institutions ended in war. The following incident shows the nature of it. My father had become President of the National Academy, and, contributing to its exhibition pictures of interest, he naturally reserved those painted by himself for his own institution. An important work was then on his easel. Aware of its destination, the managers of the Art Union instigated a connoisseur to purchase the picture, and thus prevent its exhibition by right of ownership. The plan was carried out. The connoisseur called, expressed his satisfaction with the subject, and, although informed that the painting was to be exhibited in the Academy, secured it. When completed, the picture was framed and sent to the Academy, where, according to rule, it was to remain until the exhibition closed. Just as the exhibition was about to open the purchaser claimed his property, insisted on its delivery, and finally carried things so far as to take out a writ of replevin and call in the aid of the sheriff. At this stage of the proceedings the Art Union authorities concluded to compromise the matter. The following letter, written, it must be noted, on 'April Fool's Day,' prescribed the conditions, which, indeed, transformed a serious matter into a farce :—

'NEW YORK, *April* 1, 1848.
'A. B. DURAND, ESQ.
    'SIR,—We address you as friends of Mr. ——, authorised to act for him in reference to the picture painted by you which is now

said to be in the Gallery of the Academy of Design. On behalf of Mr. —— we propose that you shall concede to him the proprietor-ship and possession of the picture, and, taking it from the Exhibition Room, place it in the frame made for it. This being done we most cheerfully, in behalf of Mr. ——, place the picture at the disposal of the National Academy for exhibition.

> ' We are,
> ' Respectfully yours,
> ' P. M. WETMORE.'

These conditions were accepted and fulfilled. The picture, removed into a side room and transferred to the frame provided for it by the owner, was then replaced in the exhibition. The incident is a sign of the times in illustration of art encourage-ment, and, again, a manifestation of the character of the artist: mild, yielding, and undemonstrative in all relations, my father in this case, and mainly in defence of the interests of the Academy, as well as of the profession, maintained his ground, notwithstanding that many of his artistic brethren, surprised at a degree of stubbornness so unusual, recommended him to consult his interests and yield. His sole revenge consisted in drawing a caricature of Art Union amateurs, which, however, remained unpublished. The ill-feeling between the institutions soon subsided. Mr. A. M. Cozzens succeeded Mr. Wetmore as president of the Art Union. In 1847 the National Academy of Design, obliged to raise money to pay off indebtedness, effected this purpose by a sale of pictures contributed by its members, which, through the good offices of Mr. Cozzens, the Art Union purchased *en masse*. Afterwards, in 1853, when the Art Union came to an end, on the discovery that it was violating the law concerning lotteries, a service of plate was presented to Mr. Cozzens in recognition of his services in the cause of American art, to which the artists of the Academy gratefully contributed. All that remains to note in connexion with the 'Art Union war' is the fate of the picture that caused the belligerent state of things. On the close of the exhibition in which it appeared, the picture was sent home. The owner, some months later, on entering his drawing-room early one morning, found the pictures on its walls cut to pieces, and this one so badly injured as to be irreparable.

The illegality of the American Art Union in no way interfered with its influence upon the progress of art. Evidence of this is found in the increase of the number of artists. In 1836 they could be counted on one's fingers; in 1851, when the Art Union fell under the ban of the law, American artists formed a large body. The collection of paintings that was to have been distributed this year, and sold at auction in 1853 to close up the institution, numbered three hundred and ninety-five works, executed by over two hundred and fifty artists, most of them born on the soil. During the period of the Art Union's existence it distributed two thousand four hundred works, besides numerous original engravings. The institution, if not the creator of a taste for art in the community, disseminated a knowledge of it and largely stimulated its growth. Through it the people awoke to the fact that art was one of the forces of society. How far the Art Union was serviceable to individual artists may be gathered from the fact that, one year, it purchased ten of my father's works.

During this period of twenty-seven years, most of the landscapes on which our artist's reputation depends were produced. The following record, accompanied with necessary comments, gives a list of them according to date and importance :—

1845. 'An Old Man's Reminiscences,' a large landscape composition, inspired by the sentiment of Goldsmith's poetry, painted for Mr. George W. Austen. Leaving his hands, it was subsequently bought by subscription for the Albany Gallery of the Fine Arts, and is now in that institution.—'Close of a Sultry Day,' of smaller dimensions, belongs to this year.

1846. 'Passage through the Woods,' painted for Mr. A. M. Cozzens: a large upright composition, the main interest of which is a vista beyond the massive trunk of a tree characteristic of local forest scenery. Novel and original in treatment, this work proved popular, and was followed in after years by others of the same order. On the sale of Mr. Cozzens' collection at his death, this picture was purchased by Mr. Morris K. Jessup, who now possesses it.—'An Old Man's Lesson,' suggested by the following well-known lines in *As You Like It :*—

> 'And this our life, exempt from public haunt,
> Finds tongues in trees, books in the running brooks,
> Sermons in stones, and good in everything.'

Purchased and distributed by the American Art Union, this work fell to the lot of a subscriber in Mobile, Ala., who sold it to Mr. E. Parmele of New Orleans.

1847. A 'Landscape Composition,' painted for Mr. Edwin Hoyt.—'Forenoon' and 'Afternoon,' for Mr. James Robb of New Orleans, lately in the Boston Museum of Art, and probably the least successful of his works.

1848. 'Dover Plains,' purchased by Mr. Daniel Seymour, and engraved by James Smillie for the American Art Union.

1849. The record of this year embraces eleven works, many of them studies from nature. Add to these a view painted for

Mr. John H. Peck, Burlington, Vt.—'Kindred Spirits,' a landscape ideal, in which the figures of Bryant and Cole appear in
the foreground on a rock; painted for Mr. Jonathan Sturges and
presented by him to Mr. W. C. Bryant.—'Indian Vespers,'
painted for Mr. Chauncey Shaffer.

1850. 'Sunday Morning,' painted for Mr. Gouverneur
Kemble, Cold Spring, inspired by Bryant's lines,—

> 'O'er the clear still water swells
> The music of the Sabbath bells,'—

and belonging to the series of tree-trunk subjects.   On its
completion, while still on the easel, Mr. Kemble writes, 'I
sent my friend Washington Irving, in whose taste I had great
confidence, to look at the picture, and have just received a note
from him expressing his admiration of it in the warmest terms.
I thought, from the pleasure it had given me, that he would be
gratified, but he has gone further than this.'—'Thanatopsis,'
again prompted by the poetry of Bryant.   Purchased by the
American Art Union, this work fell into the hands of a
subscriber, and afterwards, partially repainted by my father,
was bought by Mr. B. F. Gardner, and is now in the possession
of Mr. Pierpont Morgan. — 'Shipwreck,' painted for Mr.
Thomas H. Faile.

1851. 'Morning Ride,' painted for Mr. Jasper Grosvenor.—
'Raven Hill,' painted for Mr. John Tylor Headley.

1852. 'God's Judgment upon Gog,' the subject prescribed
by, and painted for, Mr. Jonathan Sturges.

'It represents a scene of darkness and desolation in the valley of
graves. The hosts of Gog are scattered and falling in terror, while the
blackened air is horrid with the ominous flight of birds of prey snuffing

the blood of the slain oppressors of Israel. Out of a cavernous gap in the mountains rush forth hordes of wild beasts — tigers and leopards, swift and stealthy, thirsting for blood. There is something of an awful and demoniac spirit about this scene, the widest departure from Durand's favourite themes.' *

The exhibition of this picture by the National Academy offered Mr. George William Curtis, then a young man just returned from Europe, an opportunity to exercise his critical faculty in such a way as to provoke a retort by Mr. Horatio Greenough, which the reader will find in the Appendix. It is simply necessary to state here that, as usual with subjects chosen for an artist, the picture was not a success.

1853. 'Progress,' a large landscape composition, painted for Mr. Charles Gould, showing on American soil the use of canal, steamboat, and railway, and that of the telegraph, then recently perfected.—'High Point, Shandakin,' painted for Mr. N. Ludlam, and since bequeathed by him to the Metropolitan Museum of Art, New York.

1854. 'Primeval Forest' and 'June Shower,' the former, painted for Mr. E. D. Nelson, belonging to the series of tree-trunk subjects, and the latter for Mr. H. K. Brown, both ranking among the best works that left my father's studio.

1855. 'In the Woods,' painted for Mr. Jonathan Sturges, also of the above series, and the most admired. Two years after this Mr. Sturges enclosed a cheque for two hundred dollars in a note to my father in which he says, ' I desire to add to the price of the wood picture. The trees have grown more than the worth of that sum since 1855.'—'A Summer Afternoon,' painted for Mr. J. Whiting.

* *Memorial Address.*

1856. Returning to impressions derived from Goldsmith's poetry, is 'A Symbol,' painted for Mr. R. M. Olyphant.

'An ominous storm is gathering and blackening around a mountain ; a giant peak rises high above the murky confusion below, catching a golden flush of sunlight through a rift in the clouds . . . . but the hopeful glow on the granite peak reflects more of the artist's cheerful temper than the dismal strife of the whirling clouds.' *

1857. 'Lake Hamlet,' painted for Mr. Hamilton Fish.— 'Landscape,' painted for Mr. Rollin Sanford.—'Landscape,' a tree-trunk subject, painted for Judge G. M. Speir.— 'Franconia Notch,' painted for Mr. R. L. Stuart, who, in the note enclosing a cheque for the picture, adds, 'Being much pleased with the painting, I have made the amount still more than I mentioned to you.'—Mr. Daniel Huntington painted this year the portrait of my father belonging to the Century Club. He is represented at work out of doors, sketching Mr. Stuart's picture placed on an easel, the sketch being by his own hand. The portrait, etched by James D. Smillie, forms the frontispiece of the *Memorial Address.*

1858. 'Landscape,' a large composition bearing no title, painted for Mr. L. M. Rutherford.—'New Hampshire Scenery,' painted for Mr. A. A. Low.

1859. 'A Reminiscence of the Plaaterkill Clove,' the most striking of the series of tree-trunk subjects executed by the artist, and painted for Mr. W. T. Walters. On receipt of the picture Mr. Walters writes, 'The possession of it seems to have rendered me the subject of such universal congratulation that I can assure you I feel very proud indeed. I cannot wish you better than may you live long, very long, to make such

* *Memorial Address.*

A SYCAMORE-TREE.

*Study from Nature in the Plaaterkill Clove, in the possession of
F. F. Durand. Heliogravure Dujardin. Printed by C. Wittmann.*

additions to American art, and in a profession to which your brush has added no more than your goodness and worth as a man to adorn and elevate.'

1860. 'Sunday Morning,' an ideal of American scenery, which may be considered as the culminating point of the artist's ability, painted for Mr. W. T. Walters. This work embodies all the beauty and poetry of nature, long and faithfully studied, that he was capable of putting on canvas. Mr. Walters ceded the picture to his partner, and, after the death of this gentleman, it became the property of Mr. Royal C. Taft, Providence, R.I., who now possesses it.—'Showery Day among the Mountains,' painted for the Troy Young Men's Association.

1861. 'Genesee Oaks,' painted for Mr. J. S. Wadsworth.— A landscape 'Composition,' for Mr. G. Pomeroy.

1862. 'Landscape,' painted for Mr. D. L. Bartlett, Baltimore.

At this date my father resigned the Presidency of the National Academy of Design. He was now free to pursue his labours untrammelled by public cares and duties. As Mr. Huntington states in the *Memorial Address*, he had long desired to give the office up. Fully aware that he had out-lived his generation, and that he was getting old, he was only too glad to leave the interests of artists in younger and more competent hands, and confine himself to his own works. In his sixty-seventh year his powers may have lost some of their vigour; but he was unconscious of it and still painted with the same enthusiasm. The following list of his productions from this time on to the date of his removal from the city makes the list as complete as possible. The few works he produced in his country studio will be mentioned further on.

1863. 'Lake George,' painted for Mr. B. F. Gardner,

Baltimore.   After this, for the same connoisseur, 'Hillsdale,' scenery of Columbia County, State of New York.—Landscape, 'Composition,' for Mr. H. G. Marquand.

1864. Landscape for Mr. James Cortlan, Baltimore.—'Black Mountain, Lake George,' painted for Mr. Cyrus Butler.— 'Trees,' after a study from nature made on the domain of Mr. G. C. Verplanck, Fishkill Landing, painted for the Allston Association, Baltimore.—An 'Ideal' landscape for Mr. George H. Danforth, Madison, N.J.

1865. 'Solitude,' similar in sentiment to previous pictures of forest trees, purchased by Mr. — Bruce. — 'Picnic,' painted for Mr. J. Stricker Jenkins, Baltimore.—'Santa Cruz,' painted for the Century Club, New York.—Portrait of Mr. Jonathan Sturges, for the National Academy of Design.

1866. 'Sun effect,' painted for Mr. S. P. Avery.—'Composition,' for Dr. Keener, Baltimore.

1868. 'Moonlight,' painted for Mr. B. H. Field, illustrating a poem composed by that gentleman.

1869. 'Berkshire, Massachusetts,' painted for Mr. Walter Wright, Chicago.   Destroyed in the great fire in that city, and subsequently repainted for another person.

The last work produced in this period, on which he was engaged for three years, and completed after removing to the country, was a large composition of forest trees, called 'Primeval Forest,' in which he used his most important studies from nature. The picture is now in the Corcoran Gallery, Washington.

The foregoing list of works produced in this period indicates a healthy art development in the community.   It is spontaneous and natural.   Artist and amateur meet each other without any intermediary to confirm the capacity of the one or prescribe the taste of the other ; the latter judges for himself the ability of the artist to portray real or ideal scenes which he likes, while admiration of the work when done is warmly and generously accorded. The vitality of art and the creation of an original School of Art could have no better foundation.

Productive as this period was, and professionally successful, my father cannot be said to have pursued the even tenor of his way. Domestic affliction, in the loss of his second wife in the last half of the year 1857, caused a blank in his life Again, his health gave way, mainly on account of overwork. It was at this time he sat to Rowse for a crayon portrait, in which a certain sadness of expression not characteristic of him is apparent. Time, however, the exigencies of his profession, and the natural reaction of his temperament, gradually restored his energies. The principal disturbance of his mind arose from his duties as President of the National Academy of Design, to which office he was elected in 1846, on the resignation of Professor Morse, who was absorbed by his telegraph interests. During the presidency of Mr. Morse the Academy had enjoyed a prosperous career ; its troubles began, as we have seen, in the rise of the American Art Union ; 'hard times' contributed their share, also a series of difficulties attending the procurement of a building, involving the raising of money outside the Academy's resources and, consequently, running in debt. Differences of opinion, again, occurred in the board of management, which affected the good relations of its members. This moral and business turmoil, so antipathetic to one of his temperament, worried the artist and depressed him. Even in summer, when he goes into the country for rest and to console himself as usual for all kinds of trouble by studying and painting trees,

he is not left undisturbed, as we see in the following extract
from a letter by one of his Academy associates :—

'We want you here. After this year you can stay as long
as you like in the country, but now we are struggling for
existence, and the time and talents of every member are required to preserve the independence of the profession, and keep
it from becoming the humble follower of the Art Union.
Cummings despairs entirely; but I do not if the artists will
exert themselves. The review exhibition is a dangerous experiment, and may, if not properly managed, still further involve
us; but it must be tried, for we have announced it; and no
sooner did our advertisement appear than our deadly enemies
of the Art Union put forth a notice of their forthcoming
exhibition in their new room. We want you here for several
reasons. We want you to gather in your pictures, but we want
you more particularly for the building business.'

In 1857 the war with the Art Union, as before stated,
had ceased. The Academy, mainly through friendship for its
president, had obtained funds from capitalists for purchasing
real estate and for building purposes. Things look prosperous,
and, on the opening of the exhibition this year, the favourable
prospect is celebrated by a supper, to which the friends of the
Academy and the press are invited. On this occasion, my
father, for the second and last time in his life, speaks in public,
both officially and extemporaneously, in such a way as to secure
'unbounded applause.' Unfortunately, no report of the extem-
poraneous speech exists, which is to be regretted on account of
its biographical interest. From this time on, down to 1859, the
affairs of the Academy go on smoothly. Then, however, another
building is found essential to meet the growing necessities of

the institution, as well as to secure a suitable monumental structure representing art in a city containing fine architectural productions of analogous import. Mr. Huntington, in the *Memorial Address*, treats this matter so exhaustively and sympathetically that I give way to his account of it.

'On the resignation of Professor Morse, in 1845, Durand was elected President of the Academy of Design, to which office he was unanimously re-elected till 1861. He guided the affairs of the Academy with wisdom; and the schools, exhibitions, and general affairs were successfully conducted during his energetic but conservative administration. There were troubles, however, which annoyed him. The Academy struggled with financial disasters, owing partly to business crises, partly to the distraction of free exhibitions, which diminished its receipts. We had no permanent home; the antique casts were in a hired loft, and, in order to raise money for a new building and other purposes by issuing bonds, the Academy had been obliged to place its property in the hands of trustees, of whom Durand was one.

'Difficulties arose because of conflicting ideas between the trustees and the Academy. Some urged the risking the expense of a fine building; others argued for prudence, economy, and a plain house. Durand sympathised with the artists, and strove to reconcile the opponents, but he hated turmoil, and, to secure quiet for his studies, he talked of resigning the presidency; and, notwithstanding the earnest wishes of the members, he did so in 1861. Some time before this, a circumstance occurred which furnished an occasion for the resignation he had contemplated. Proposals had been made for a new building on Twenty-third Street. Plans were invited from a few architects, and a time fixed for their presentation for decision by the

Council. On the evening of the appointed day the Council
assembled. President Durand was in the chair. The designs
of the competing architects were displayed, but only two were
judged worthy of serious consideration. Of these, one was by
an architect then well known for his practical skill, but was
thought too plain and commonplace in its effect to the eye.
The other was by Eidlitz, in the Palladian style, pleasing and
appropriate. Durand decidedly favoured the latter. Most of
us agreed with him, and after discussion we voted to accept it.
This decision was not absolutely final, the consent of the trustees
being necessary. We adjourned, and President Durand went
home. No sooner had he left than the officer in charge of the
designs said : "Gentlemen, there is another drawing, but as it
came after the time fixed for receiving designs had passed, I
have not thought it proper to place it in competition." We
exclaimed against so much "red tape," and asked to see it. It
was brought out. It was a design by Wight, very much like
our building as it now stands, but more beautiful and picturesque.
We called for a reorganization. The Vice-President took the
chair; we reconsidered the previous vote, and almost unanimously
decided for Wight's design.

'Our excitement, and the vexation at the withholding of
the best design, betrayed us into this lawless disrespect to our
honoured President. As one of the culprits, I may say it was
outrageous, and Durand was justly indignant. We apologised;
the whole body of Academicians joined in a petition, but he never
took the chair again.

'I must say that, though he was resolute in refusing to
condone this unmannerly proceeding of ours in his official
capacity, he was personally as kind and friendly as ever to

every one of us; if possible, even more so. I believe he was glad to escape from the anxiety and responsibility of the presidency, and resume the even tenor of his studious life.

'I am confident he was happier, and grateful for an occurrence which furnished him with a good opportunity of retiring. He wished to do so some time before, but felt bound to remain in the office on account of the large amount of money which his two friends, Jonathan Sturges and Chas. M. Leupp, had loaned to the Academy, in great measure out of personal regard to him, and on bonds which Durand had signed as President, and for the payment of which he felt an honourable responsibility.'

More must be said of the summer sojourns in the country, forming, as they do, important episodes of my father's professional career, and, besides this, furnishing details of his ways, habits, and thoughts. His first object was always to study from nature. After the toil of the winter months both vigour of mind and body required restoration at the fountain-head of his inspiration. Hoboken no longer offered picturesque opportunities. Generally speaking, these country expeditions led him to seek wild regions, before railways had penetrated to their recesses, where only a few scattered inhabitants could be found, almost as primitive as the forests, lakes, streams, and mountains around them. He visited, according to opportunity and as facilities for travel by main lines increased, every region in the North supposed to be pictorially available; always branching off to escape civilisation, ever ready to 'rough it' over corduroy, muddy, or sandy roads, in stage-coach and on 'buck-boards,' to the great weariness of the flesh; stopping in the wilderness wherever the forms and colour of rocks, the trunks and branching of particular trees, the verdant masses of middle-distance, and the lines of the mountains answered to his search for the beautiful. The following places visited by him, at which he sojourned for weeks or months according to their respective attractions, show his familiarity with the scenery of his country. The banks of the Hudson River, near home, like Hoboken in early years, come first in order—' Jacob's Valley,' at Kingston ; then, farther west, every nook, corner, and ' clove' in the Catskill, Shandakin, and Shawangunk mountains ; after these, to the north, Lake George with Lake Champlain and its shores, the Adirondacks on one side and the mountains of Vermont on the other ; then, to the east, the White Mountains, North Conway, West Campton, the Berkshire Hills in Massachusetts, the Valley of the Connecticut, and again Lake George for many seasons, all so many ' haunts of nature' in the delineation of whose beauties his brush never grew weary.

Generally, his family accompanied him on these excursions. In early years his pupil, Mr. Casilear, was his sole companion. As time went on and a younger generation of artists grew up, they would join him. Among these must be mentioned Kensett, Cranch, Addison Richards, Hotchkiss, Hubbard, Alfred Jones, David Johnson, Hall, and others ; E. D. Nelson, an amateur, and the only pupil who worked in his studio; and Miss Josephine Walters, whom he often advised in the pursuit of her studies.

Owing to the difficulty of procuring comfortable quarters, good food, and good beds, in farmhouses and at country taverns on these summer excursions, my father was induced in 1849 to try a suburban residence of his own. He accordingly purchased, near Newburg, on the Hudson River, a house situated on an elevation overlooking the ' Vale of Avoca,' through which ran

A BUTTERNUT-TREE.

Study from Nature on Lake George, in the possession of J. Durand.
Heliogravure Dujardin. Printed by C. Wittmann.

a somewhat picturesque stream. Unfortunately, romance yielded to reality. The banks of the stream ' meandering through the vale' were soon wanted for a railroad ; the ground was turned up ; fever-and-ague made its appearance, drove him from his country retreat, and obliged him to resume his annual search for the picturesque in the undisturbed wilderness.

These excursions were in no sense pleasure trips. Discomforts and privations of all kinds awaited him at every turn, and were cheerfully accepted. The obligations and proprieties of society, too—regarded as annoyances which interfered with work—were always, when it was possible, avoided, as we see in the following extract from a letter written in 1843, dated at a certain place too civilised for his purposes :—

' We are all well here, except that I have a slight indisposition in consequence of visits and parties, from all of which in future I am sworn off—except one that takes place to-night at our house, from which I cannot well escape. I begin to be sick of the place, solely on account of society, and if I knew where to transport myself out of the way of such a nuisance, I would do it forthwith ; but I conclude to remain and conceal myself in the woods when I can't in the house.'

His own letters, as well as those by members of his family, afford glimpses of the privations endured in those places, also of amusements and of the society that he liked. Writing in October 1848, from Palensville, at the entrance of the Catskill Clove, he says, ' The Clove is rich in beautiful wildness beyond all we have met with heretofore. . . . . With the exception of two days, the weather has been so cold that we have worked in overcoats and overshoes, and, in addition, have been obliged to have a constant fire alongside for an occasional warming, all of

B B

which I have endured pretty well, with no worse effect than a slight cold.'   At another place he says, 'I caught a fine trout which I ate for breakfast—the only decent one I have had since I came here ; sour bread, salt pork, and ham being the staple commodities.'

'Besides Casilear and Kensett,' writes one of the family, 'we have Mr. Volmering, the Dane, with us, or, at least, next door, so that we have plenty of talk—amusing, bad English—and smoking every evening.   You will see that, although retired, we are not lonesome. . . . . The bar-room does all it can to lighten our troubles.   Wet floors are disagreeable and tobacco smoke in a close room unpleasant, but we all put on the best face and contribute our mite to the general fund of amusement, playing cards indoors when it rains, and, out of doors, singing and guessing conundrums, our stock of which is so exhausted that we shall have to exercise our faculties in some other fashion. Our amusements are all of the quiet kind except one, with which every new-comer, friend or stranger, is, in our lawlessness, generally greeted.   Each of the party is assigned a separate syllable of a particular sound, which, at a given signal, is vociferously expressed, the result being one grand *sneeze* especially astonishing to strangers.   I leave you to imagine what the effect would be were you to enter a room containing twelve or fifteen persons of different ages, some so quiet and grave in appearance as to preclude the suspicion of a joke, and find them all at once joining in a deafening sneeze and suddenly bursting out in a laugh at your astonishment!'

At Geneseo (1856) he is annoyed by the poor quality of colours and canvases ; he writes, ' With all my trouble I believe I have learned more of the management of colours in the painting of tones than by all my previous practice, although I have never produced so little in the same space of time, having made only four studies in five weeks.' An examination of these studies shows minute drawing, unsurpassed in those made in other places.

One season my father and Mr. Casilear happened to be studying nature in the valley of the Mohawk, during the anti-rent troubles on the Van Rensselaer estate. Provided with camp-stools, easels, and other sketching paraphernalia, they found themselves watched by masked men for some days, and finally were told that they must decamp, as *surveyors* were not allowed there!

Knowing the desire of the painter for picturesque spots, his friends would often recommend this or that place, as they thought it adapted to his studies. It is curious to note in this connexion that, with most of them, the picturesque was always an extensive prospect. Among letters of this kind, I find one written from a prosperous city west of the Alleghanies and which now contains collections of paintings worthy of note. The writer is on his travels in the year 1853, and, apparently, in search of works of art. The painting he alludes to was a supposed 'old master.'

'I hope you will excuse the liberty I take in addressing you respecting an old oil painting I have picked up in this land of hogs, corn, and negroes. How it came here I know not. We have here people from every part of Europe—German, Swiss, Dutch, French, Spanish, and Italian. I find the natives here have no taste for the Fine Arts—'tis like throwing "pearls before swine"—but for a fine mule, a fat hog, or a fine stout negro, who will readily bring $1000, they have a pretty considerable relish. Flesh and blood, both of man and beast, will always bring ready cash; paint and canvas are much below par. Some of your

Eastern artists, who paint by steam, have made several trials here at auction. A lot of one hundred and fifty works, with elegant gold-looking frames and plenty of red, blue, and yellow paint, were offered the other day; about four or five people who appeared to be buyers attended. A few pictures were knocked down, perhaps to sham bidders, at a less price than the cost of the frames. The owner, if wise, will never try again. Half-a-dozen might sell at Christmas or New Year, which would suffice for twelve months.'

These details furnish a sort of background to artistic life in the woods. A few words are here pertinent in relation to the studies from nature, the fruit of all these varied experiences. An artist once visited the studio of my father in the city, and, after carefully examining his studies, exclaimed, ' Mr. Durand, where did you find such trees?' He replied, designating one of the principal forest regions or the State of New York. ' Well,' said the visitor, ' I have been all over those woods, and I never saw trees like these!'—for the reason, perhaps, that perceptions or insight differ, or, which is most probable, methods of study. My father's practice was, while faithfully painting what he saw, not to paint all that he saw. Finding trees in groups, he selected one that seemed to him, in age, colour, or form, to be the most characteristic of its species, or, in other words, the most beautiful. In painting its surroundings, he eliminated all shrubs and other trees which interfered with the impression made by this one. Every outdoor study, as well as every pictorial composition, was regarded as a sort of dramatic scene in which a particular tree or aspect of nature may be called the principal figure ; other trees, as in the case of a study, being subordinate and of relative value in giving the most interesting object strong relief. To him, certain objects and aspects were more beautiful than others, and not

AN OAK-TREE.

Study from Nature on the Domain of Gulian C. Verplanck, near Fishkill Landing, Hudson River, in the possession of Robert Hoe, Esq. Heliogravure Dujardin. Printed by C. Wittmann.

so many details to be servilely and indiscriminately imitated.*

We must now turn to other matters belonging to this period. In 1858 the writer, jointly with Mr. W. J. Stillman, had the misfortune to embark in a journalistic enterprise called the *Crayon*, devoted to art and its interests. It proved unsuccessful. To a man of large income, wishing to amuse himself in the way in which another would run a yacht without regard to expense, the venture might be termed practicable ; but to one who relied on a paying sympathy for art in the community it was a Quixotic undertaking, the folly of which needed only experience to make intelligible. To help this enterprise my father wrote for the *Crayon* a series of ' Letters on Landscape Painting.' Hastily composed in his leisure moments, and somewhat ' against the grain,' as literary efforts were now out of his line, these letters have some interest on account of his observations on the study of art and nature, as well as giving an account of his methods in painting.

The rise of the American school of art has been exhibited to a certain extent on the foregoing pages. Springing out of the instinct for art common to all people who use objects in nature to make the meaning of ideas and emotions widely understood, it has its right to a place among the schools of the world. Some of the influences stimulating its growth and establishment have been traced. Up to the end of the period with which we are now concerned, the school may be said to have prospered, although a decrease of its prosperity becomes apparent at an earlier date. The professional career of my father indicates the period of its prosperity. At the end of

* See ' Letters on Landscape Painting,' in the Appendix.

his career, its decline is marked.   The causes of this decline
are easily pointed out.

The American school of art begins with portraiture — a
favourite branch of art with the Anglo-Saxons.*   Colonial in
its origin, it is the art of the country down to the advent of
Luman Reed, when landscape art begins to flourish.   Very few
artists of that day, however, represent the practice of this
branch of art.   In the succeeding generation landscapists multiply
speedily, which indicates an expansion of public taste.   Historic
and other departments of ideal art also make their appearance.
The diversity and talent of the school at this epoch, to those
familiar with the society and scenery of the country which
inspires the artistic mind, is represented by the names of certain
painters, sculptors, and engravers, taken haphazard :—Huntington, Gray, Cheney, Casilear, Kensett, Darley, Ehninger, Rossiter,
Woodville, Baker, Church, Elliott, Bierstadt, Gifford, Whittredge, McEntee, Beard, William Hart, James Hart, Shattuck,
George Lambdin, David Johnson, Bristol, Hubbard, Colman,
Mignot, Hotchkiss, Leutze, F. B. Mayer, Eastman Johnson, and
many others among the painters ; of the sculptors, Greenough,

* 'In England, portrait-painting, which touched another sentiment besides
love of pure art, was the only form that was really encouraged.   Painter after
painter, distinguished in other branches, came over to England, but they in-
variably found that they could succeed only by devoting themselves to the one
department which appealed directly to the vanity of their patrons. . . . "Painters
of history," says Kneller, "make the dead live, but do not begin themselves to
live until they are dead.   I paint the living, and they make me live." . . . No
painter, however excellent, can succeed among the English that is not engaged
in painting portraits. . . . Hogarth described portrait-painting as "the only
flourishing branch of the high tree of British art."'   Canaletti, Vanloo, Watteau,
and Van Dyck, all famous in other branches, had to paint portraits on coming
to England.   Lecky calls this the 'darkest period of British art.'   See *History
of England in. the Eighteenth Century,* text and foot-notes, vol. i., page 529.

Power, Rogers, Bartholomew, Ives, Ball, H. K. Brown, and E. D. Palmer ; of the engravers, Danforth, John Cheney, Smillie, Jones, Schoff, Burt, and Marshall. Each artist, it must be noted, has a style of his own—a style entirely personal, due to original perceptions and impressions of external nature, as well as of dramatic or pictorial elements belonging to local social experiences.

Unfortunately the American school of art is an invisible factor among literary and other intellectual products of the country. As far as native productions are concerned, they are scattered over the country, hidden away in private houses and displayed in gloomy drawing-rooms, where sunlight scarcely ever penetrates; colours here fade for want of light, and canvases moulder under coatings of dust, damp, and gaseous exhalations. Rarely do the owners lend them for public exhibitions. Even when American works find their way out of private collections before the public, or, again, are purchased by local institutions, they are hung in proximity to works of older schools, inspired by different sentiments and executed according to different methods : American art thus suffers by comparison, the same as the art of all modern schools suffers more or less by contact with the masterpieces of the old masters. Introduce a Rembrandt, a Raphael, a Velasquez, a Titian, or any work of a great genius of the Renaissance epoch into the finest modern collection, and all other works grow pale before it. What America needs is a public gallery (like Kensington Museum in London), where the works of American artists can be seen by themselves, separate from all other schools and taken for what they are—the fresh outcome of feeling and thought inspired by a nature needing new interpreters.*

* What the effect of a gallery of this order would be, may be estimated

But it is not my purpose to enforce a special consideration of the American school of art. It is sufficient to state to those who have not arrived at a proper appreciation of it, that if the country possesses able men of marked capacity, types of intellectual achievement in other directions—if the country is proud of a Hamilton, a Clay, a Webster among statesmen ; a Cooper, an Irving, a Bryant, a Parkman among literary magnates ; a Fulton among inventors, a Henry among scientists—it has equal right to be proud of a Stuart, a Vanderlyn, a Trumbull, an Allston, and a Cole among the artists.

We have now to dwell for a moment on the decline of the prosperity of the American school of art at the end of this period. Its growth has been attributed to the fostering influence of the commercial spirit which rules in the community ; its decline is due to the withdrawal of this fostering influence, diverted away from it by the introduction into the country of foreign art. The causes of this can be only briefly and summarily stated.

The eclipse of American art may be said to begin with the establishment of the Dusseldorf Gallery in New York in 1849, a gallery which owes its existence to Mr. John G. Boker, a resident in Dusseldorf for twenty years, and afterwards Prussian consul in the city of New York. Intimate with the artists of Dusseldorf, and divining probably, with true commercial sagacity, that America might prove a good market for their works, and probably, again, influenced by Leutze, who, although born in this country, was to all intents and purposes a Dusseldorf artist, Mr. Boker obtained a fine collection of their works and placed

by the fine private collection of works wholly by American artists made by Mr. T. B. Clarke in New York, a worthy successor of Luman Reed.

it before the New York public. The exhibition proved a success, but not in the way of sales. The Dusseldorf school had no prestige, and, besides this, the public were not prepared for it either intellectually or financially. Some people regarded the pictures as either painted by, or belonging to, a 'Mr. Dusseldorf.' All it denotes is the first appearance amongst us of foreign art on a large scale.

The private collection of Mr. John Wolfe comes next in its influence—a collection largely Dusseldorf, and well known among local amateurs. The gradual increase of French pictures introduced into the country indicates the spread of taste in that direction. The first French work which excited the public mind was 'The Horse Fair,' painted by Rosa Bonheur, and purchased by Mr. W. P. Wright for seven thousand dollars. Here the sensational elements necessary for stimulating public curiosity were at hand—a work notorious in Europe, produced by a woman, and for which more thousands of dollars were given for a mere painting than ever before by a private individual in America. The Press took up the theme, and spread the fame of 'The Horse Fair' far and near, aided by romantic details of the artist's life. Next came a French work of kindred interest, 'The Duel,' by Gérôme, bought by Mr. W. T. Walters of Baltimore. It must be here stated that, at this time, the public mind in America had been quickened in relation to art by the writings and teachings of Ruskin. Whatever may be said of the criticisms of works of art, ancient and modern, by this eminent writer, of his estimate of special genius, of his theories, hobbies, and idiosyncrasies, it is certain that he developed more interest in art in the United States than all other agencies put together. His remarkable word-painting, the theological bent of his mind, his ascetic temperament, his eccentricities, his moral injunctions, furnishing both pulpit and press with material for sermons, news, and gossip about art, making popular music on the three strings of the mental harp to which the public ear is sensitive, spread a knowledge of art among people who would not otherwise have given it a thought.   Ruskin himself, in his extreme admiration of the works of Edouard Frère, gave an immense impetus to the popularity of the French school.   But Ruskin's influence was confined to the intellect ; we have to do with the pocket.   Two well-advertised works that excited the taste of the rich have already been mentioned.   To these may be added the fine collection of foreign works belonging to Mr. August Belmont. In the times of pre-Raphaelitism, an English collection came to this country and met with partial success, but not enough to render English art popular among picture - buyers.   The inundation remained wholly French, increased rapidly, and finally culminated in a ' craze ' that led to the purchase of Meissonier's ' Charge of Cavalry ' for sixty thousand dollars, and, at last, of ' The Angelus ' by Millet for one hundred thousand dollars.

Of course this great influx of foreign art could not have occurred without a corresponding expansion of wealth at home. Beginning in the East, the wave of wealth rolled onward to the Pacific.   Through the profits of mines, railway enterprises, and cattle-raising, it ran mountain high.   A new generation of energetic men indifferent to Eastern ideals spring up, and, craving new outlets for the expenditure of their fortunes as well as new criterions of social distinction, find these in the adoption of a taste for art.   Western millionaires begin to buy French pictures right and left.   Entering the markets of New

York and Paris, they vie with each other and with their Eastern rivals in seeing who could pay dearest for recognised master-pieces. Other agencies help this *furore* along. Picture-dealers, exercising the most influence, find in foreign art a gold-mine. Realising profits of one, two, and three hundred per cent. on the works that pass through their hands, they serve as inter-mediaries between patron and artist, and keep the interest at fever heat. The Press push on a cause equally fertile in news items and sensational phenomena. Native students, finding foreign art in the ascendant, abandon original perceptions and imitate the methods and aims of a foreign school. Add to this the one-sided admiration of this or that French 'Master' whose life and career offer romantic episodes, ludicrously exaggerated in the eyes of those familiar with the facts, and we have a remarkable combination of influences which fully explain the disappearance of local art—like houses and bridges swept away in a mountain torrent. The American school becomes out of fashion, and is even derided by native writers. It is gravely asserted by one of these that there was no American school previous to the founding of the Metropolitan Museum in New York, while another asserts that it did not come into existence until a much later period.

In thus attributing the decline of the American school of art to the diversion of the native patronage which once ensured its development, I do not deprecate or depreciate the result. On the contrary, one cannot too highly esteem the introduction into the country of foreign treasures of art of incalculable value in every sense. Whoever wishes, indeed, to fully estimate French art of this generation, can do it better in America than in France, for most of its masterpieces are in our land. My object is simply to explain a fact in the history of American art—the eclipse of the American school, not yet at an end. Fortunately, this eclipse is only temporary. Natural instincts for art depending on American genius, patronage, and surroundings, will yet assert themselves. The community will sooner or later demand from its artists a conformity to the nature around them, and an interpretation of it not according to foreign standards of beauty or methods of execution, but as they really see and feel it according to original and common impulses.

CHAPTER XII.

THE principal incidents and experiences of my father's professional life are narrated ; we have now to follow him into the country, where he passed the remainder of his days. Apart from his taste for rural life and the desire for repose natural at his age, he was obliged to leave the city on account of annoyances which rendered the neighbourhood of his home extremely disagreeable. He had passed fifty-four years in the metropolis, and thirty-one of these in Amity Street. When he established himself in 1832 in this street, it was on the outskirts of the city, far above business tumult and fashion. In 1869 it was 'down-town ;' fashion had arrived at and long abandoned the vicinity, while the immediate neighbourhood had been invaded by foreign artisans not remarkable for cleanliness or morality, occupying tenement - houses and the dilapidated mansions of their predecessors. A retreat became imperative. As it is dangerous to disturb a man seventy-three years of age, accustomed to a certain routine, the problem consisted in how to break up the confirmed habits of a veteran and establish a new home for him in which the comforts and conveniences of the old could be maintained. A transfer to an entirely new locality without associations of some kind was not to be thought of. Fortunately, the family property at Jefferson Village (now Maplewood) in New Jersey, near South Orange, belonged to him, and was considered the most eligible place. Being his birthplace and familiar ground, he would not be obliged to accustom himself to new scenes and new society. The old house in which he was born having been destroyed by fire, a new one was erected on its site, provided with a larger studio and a finer light than his former one in the city, and to this he removed in April 1869. His favourite studies from nature, arranged on its walls, surrounded him, and it was not long before he was at his easel as if his labours had never been interrupted. The residence of his son-in-law, Mr. George Woodman, built the same time as his own a short distance toward the mountain, furnished him with a convenient stopping-place on his daily walks, and likewise pleasant chats with his daughter and grand-children. At home the rest of his children lived with him and relieved him of all household cares. Not far off an artist, Mr. Gaston Fay, resided, while on the opposite side of the road there soon came Dr. Alfred M. Mayer, of the Stevens Institute, with his family. Add to these the always welcome calls of his old pupil, Rev. Dr. Clover, and those of his physician, Dr. Whittingham, who fully replaced Dr. J. C. Peters, his regretted medical adviser in the city, and he enjoyed a society which left nothing to be desired.

The few works executed by him during this final period of his career sum up the labour of his life. The picture of 'Primeval Forest,' mentioned as belonging to the Corcoran Gallery, and still at this time (1870) unfinished, first engaged his attention. This received its final touches in the country studio. After completing this work, he painted one or two portraits and two small landscapes. The last picture of any size produced by him is a 'View on Lake George,' still in the possession of the family. In 1876 he produced a work called 'Sunset on Chocorua,' purchased by Mr. J. B. Dod, of Hoboken.

In 1873 my father, commissioned to paint a certain subject by a gentleman who gave such minute instructions in the matter as greatly to worry him, addressed the following letter to him, giving some of his views in relation to painting by prescription :—

'I have made all the alterations in the picture suggested by you that I deem advisable. As to the picture meeting your approval, I must add that it gratifies me to have those who possess my works pleased with them ; at the same time, in executing them, I cannot consult their taste beyond my own in the matter of artistic completeness. Every condition on which I undertook the picture has been fulfilled ; but not wishing to urge it on you, and likewise unwilling to wait until it may be convenient to you to take it, I request that you will advise me by the fifth of February next whether you will accept it as it is ; after that date I shall consider myself at liberty to dispose of it to another party.'

An answer came to the following effect :—

'As you think you can dispose of the picture to another person, I would suggest whether it might not be well for you to do so and paint another for me. . . . In another effort there is but little doubt you would be able to satisfy me fully.'

Declining this proposal, the picture found a resting-place elsewhere.

Time was dealing gently with the venerable artist during these last years of his professional career. He enjoyed his work as much as ever, his mind remaining clear and his faculties apparently unimpaired; most of his morning hours were passed in his studio, the rest of the day being devoted as heretofore to repose and exercise. Nevertheless, the strength which had enabled him to pursue his labours so satisfactorily was gradually giving way. His last picture, as is stated in the *Memorial Address*, painted in 1879, was a 'Souvenir of the Adirondacks' —a sunset, in which the softly suffused light, spreading over a placid lake and quiet sky, aptly figures the tranquility of his closing years. As he made the last touches to this picture with a hand enfeebled by the weight of eighty-three years, he laid down his palette and brushes for ever, saying that 'his hand would no longer do what he wanted it to do.' This was a day to which his friends and family had looked forward with apprehension. But their fears proved groundless. Accepting the situation with his usual equanimity and unconscious that art was for him a thing of the past, he left his studio without a sign of depression, scarcely ever returned to it, and resumed his rambles on the mountain, apparently content with nature as he enjoyed it in his boyhood. Nothing in his manner or bearing indicated a want of occupation, or that he felt he had abandoned one on which the even tenor of his life depended.

The reader may have remarked on these pages the many evidences of good feeling and esteem for my father on the part of his brethren of the profession. In 1854 a compliment had been paid him by the body of artists and other friends in the shape of a service of plate. Soon after his withdrawal to his new home in the country, in 1872, three years after leaving the city, another manifestation of the same import was made which, on account of its novel character, deserves special mention. Mr. Jervis McEntee in his boyhood had consulted my father in relation to the pursuit of art, and, having been eminently successful, suggested to his brother artists a ' surprise party,' consisting of a picnic in the woods of Maplewood, the material for which in the shape of refreshments was to be carried along with them from the city. The idea was approved of, and a committee appointed, consisting of Messrs. McEntee, Huntington, S. R. Gifford, Kensett, and Hall, to carry it out. The 8th of June was selected for the occasion.* The morning was rainy; before noon, however, the sky cleared and the day proved charming. Nevertheless, the ground being wet, and the house capacious enough for the festivity, the woods were abandoned, while the lunch, spread on a table on the veranda, took place with the usual toasts, speeches, and general hilarity characteristic of an informal gathering and where none are strangers. Mr. Bryant, a friend for more than forty years, made a graceful address, followed by a feeling response on the part of him whom all delighted to honour. Mr. Page, whose love for Shakespeare's sonnets seemed irrepressible, availed himself of every chance to rise and repeat one of these in spite of the amusing efforts of

---

* There were present at this party Mr. William Cullen Bryant, Mr. and Mrs. Wm. Page, Mr. and Mrs. McEntee, Mr. and Mrs. Eastman Johnson, Mr. and Mrs. Thomas Hicks, Mr. J. F. Kensett, Mr. and Mrs. E. D. Palmer, Mr. Brevoort, Miss Bascom (afterwards Mrs. Brevoort), Mr. W. Whittredge, Mr. Launt Thompson, Mr. C. P. Cranch, Mr. J. Q. A. Ward, Mr. G. H. Hall, and Mr. J. M. Falconer. Mr. Huntington (prevented by illness), Mr. Alfred Jones, and Mr. H. K. Brown, were to have been of the number ; also, as historiographet, Mr. John R. Thompson, but who, in delicate health, was prevented from coming by the threatening aspect of the weather.

Messrs. Hicks and Kensett, on either side, to keep him in his seat. Others gave stories and souvenirs of the past. Two of the ladies being accomplished pianists, music followed in the drawing-room, after which walks in the woods and on the mountain, until, towards evening, the party, whirled off to the railway station behind four-horse teams, gave many and loud cheers on bidding adieu to the venerable subject of their kind ovation. Mr. McEntee thus characterises the festivity in a general way in a letter to a friend: 'The picnic was a perfect success. . . . . It was a most satisfactory day, and I shall always remember with gratification that my suggestion was so heartily responded to, and that we were able to show in so fitting a way our veneration for the old man.' Another evidence of this veneration is supplied, in this connexion, in a letter to Mr. McEntee from Mr. John F. Weir, resident at New Haven, and unable to attend:—

'As to the designed honour and professional esteem for Mr. Durand, with that I heartily sympathise. I think we do too little, and cannot do too much, to show our respect for the pioneers of our pathways which have now become highways. I could sympathise with nothing more heartily than with this, and I hope that you will not count me absent in spirit when you are deep in the " champagne" libations. . . . You are sure of having a glorious time, and in honouring Durand all you "landscape fellows" honour yourselves.'

Many were the applications of young men to him during his career for advice in the pursuit of art. In every case, and always mindful of his early trials, he replied with all the fulness and clearness that he could. In fact, it is these applications which prompted his 'Letters on Landscape Painting,' published in the *Crayon*, and previously alluded to. As a fitting close to manifestations of this kind, I give a letter from Mr. Jared B.

Flagg, kindly answering my request for any souvenirs of my father that he might possess :—

'My Dear Mr. Durand,

'My relations to your father, though not intimate, have left pleasing and valued memories. It is now more than fifty years since I, a young art-student, called at his studio in Duane Street. I was from New Haven, Conn., and a total stranger in New York. It was quite an event for a lad of sixteen to call and introduce himself to a distinguished artist! I well remember my emotions at the time. I was embarrassed with a feeling of awe and diffidence as I rang the bell and waited the opening of the door. Your father received me with a gentle cordiality of manner that soon placed me at my ease. I told him I had heard so often of him as the engraver of Vanderlyn's "Ariadne," and as a painter, that I was desirous to see him, and that I esteemed it a great privilege to be admitted to his studio. He was full of the spirit of the true artist, and the hour I spent with him was both pleasant and profitable. He met my artistic enthusiasm as one deeply interested in my success, and seemed to take pleasure in answering numerous questions which I propounded relating to modes and methods of painting. I carried from his studio the impression of a man of great simplicity, sincerity, and amiability.

'A few years after this interview I came to New York to reside, and occupied a studio on Broadway not far from your father's residence. My success, which was very encouraging, was largely due to his interest in my behalf. To persons inquiring for a portrait-painter, he would give my name with words of commendation that carried great weight of influence. Mr. Tileston, a man of wealth, interested in a line of trans-Atlantic steamers, and a lover of art, offered to give to any artist, desiring to study abroad, whom your father, then President of the National Academy of Design, would nominate, a free passage to Europe. In the second year of my residence in New York, I was honoured as your father's nominee, but was unable to avail myself of the privilege. Such kindly interposition for my advancement laid me under an obligation of gratitude in which I shared with many others, for he was one who loved to aid his fellow-men. I do not think that he had an enemy, and when in the fulness of years he passed on to the higher life, the benediction of a circle far wider than that of his family, or the community in which he lived, followed him.

'It is eminently proper that such men should be embalmed in our literature, and kept fresh in the memory of succeeding generations by special biographical memorial. They are the common property of the race, and I know of no more beneficent work than that of giving them such prominence, that they who came after them may draw from the record of their virtues, inspiration and encouragement.'

I add one more testimonial of this description furnished by Mr. S. P. Avery, familiar with the artist's career in all directions :—

' As for me, I like to talk with those who knew him, and thus refresh my recollections of him—always kind to me, so simple in his manners and in his ways of life, so modest in his claims to fame, so sound in his judgment of art, such a helper to all seeking for information, so strong in the right, so generous in his recognition of rising talent, so thoroughly an American in the good old-time sense.'

Notwithstanding the removal to the country, the usual summer excursion was not abandoned. My sister, who always accompanied my father on these occasions, states :—

' We went twice to the Adirondacks and seven times to Lake George after we removed to Maplewood, the last excursion being in 1877, in his eighty-first year. We camped out twice, once at the Ausable and again at Lake Placid. As it was the first experiment of the kind with him, we were anxious about the result. But it turned out well. We hung his corner of the tent with rubber blankets, and covered his bed of spruce or balsam boughs with a buffalo robe, and though it rained hard three nights there were no bad effects from it. Good camp-fires in front of the tent, being so much in the pure air, and good meals, kept him well. It was then that he made the studies for the picture now on the easel in the studio, and his last work.'

A PINE-TREE.

Study from Nature on Lake George, in the possession of
F. F. Durand. Heliogravure Dujardin. Printed by C. Wittmann.

On one of these excursions, Mr. Huntington encountered him, as mentioned in the *Memorial Address*, and thus alludes to it : —

'Durand was fond of Lake George scenery, and there painted many of his best studies. I visited the pleasant resort he frequented late in the afternoon, as the shadows were deepening in the ravines of Black Mountain. We were kindly welcomed by the white-haired artist, who was smoking his quiet pipe on the old-fashioned stoop of the snug farm-house, surrounded by a group of friends and members of his family. The following day we made a party to row to Harbour Island for sketches and a picnic. It was a lovely day in the early autumn. Harbour Island is one of the beauties of Lake George—irregular in shape, varied by forests and rocky shores, having a sequestered interior bay with a narrow entrance, where the still, transparent water, protected from wind, reflects every leaf. Durand, with his accustomed industry, was soon busy with a study. Some sketched or strolled about, or lounged with idle oars to various points of the shore. The views are beautiful. To the east rises the massive form of Black Mountain ; to the south stretches the lake, dotted by the hundred islands of the Narrows ; and the western outlook is hemmed in by the broken outline, deep forests, and rocky precipices of Tongue Mountain. In this fascinating region Durand calmly but earnestly pursued his summer studies for several seasons. The serene, translucent waters of Lake George were typical of the frank, placid, and truthful spirit of the man.'

After he stopped painting his energies relaxed somewhat, and he was content to remain at home. It might be supposed that time would hang heavy on his hands, but this was not the case. Early in life, before he relinquished engraving, he had acquired a knowledge of French, which at this period proved a great resource. He read nearly all the works of Renan and of Taine, then appearing, and in the *Revue Germanique* found a large collection of tales and romances. He always preferred reading to himself instead of being read to. Most of his hours in summer were passed on the veranda of his house, seated in the sunshine, smoking his pipe and watching the life on the road before him.   Here he received the calls of his neighbours and occasional visitors from the city.   I am indebted to Dr. Mayer, his nearest neighbour, for the following reminiscence, showing the humorous side of the artist's character.   My father's aversion to the intrusive interviewer, without know-ledge and with still less delicacy, who has no scruples in speculating on private feelings or opinions, was very great. Dr. Mayer found him engaged with one of those individuals, questioning him on behalf of a certain health journal.

'Mr. Durand, I suppose that you never used tobacco?'

'Yes, sir, I have always used it; I smoke now, and when a young man I chewed.'

'Ah! but you did not drink ardent spirits.   How is that?'

'Yes, sir, I have, and do so now.   My daughter has just given me an egg-nogg with brandy in it.'

'Well, during your long life you have done a deal of work?'

'That is true.   I have spoiled a great many canvases.'

After this the interviewer, somewhat disconcerted, withdrew, the information he obtained in no respect answering to his fore-gone conclusions.

I add other reminiscences of the closing years of his life furnished by Mr. Barnet Phillips in an appreciative article already quoted from:—

'Mr. Durand states that his scepticism in regard to maps and their accuracy dates from an early period, a person who had left a map for him to engrave having complained of the omission in it of a certain large river; requested to show where the river might be, he placed his broad finger on a large county and observed, " Put it here, the river runs some-

where about there." Alluding to the abandonment of engraving for
painting, "What a relief it was," said Mr. Durand, with youthful ex-
pansiveness, "to be able to stand for an hour before some fine tree, in
direct sympathy with it! I had done so when a boy, on long summer
days, and now, when a man, I had a higher appreciation of it than
ever, and enjoyed it all the more—the great happiness of standing face
to face with nature!"'

We now reach the closing years of his life. Enough has been
given on these pages, it is hoped, to enable the reader to form
some idea of the artist's temperament, habits, and disposition.
One or two details may be added. In a country where self-
interest is pushed to extremity, my father was an exception ;
personal interests, as far as these depended on any form of
self-assertion, were lost sight of. This absence of a calculating
spirit was accompanied with an even temper, never ruffled by
misfortune or disappointment. Losses, failures, afflictions, and
sacrifices always were accepted with unquestioning resignation.
If occasionally roused by some attack on his dignity or conscience, his resentment was never of long duration. The same
serenity and equanimity continued to the last hour. Free from
organic disease, the last six years of his life passed away exempt
from suffering, and attended with no discomfort except that
which necessarily accompanies the decline of faculties impaired
by age. Unworldly in every sense, with no longing unsatisfied,
no work that he had projected unfinished, no expression ever
denoted a regret in relation to the past or betokened any kind
of mental despondency. Day after day passed tranquilly,
without loss of interest, according to the state of his faculties,
in persons or things around him. Surrounded by his children
and grandchildren, every want and feeling gratified, he thus

glided gently along until the final hour was reached. Those who loved him have the satisfaction of knowing that his life ended in an honoured, happy, and beautiful old age.

It is not in my province to estimate the professional capacity or the character of the man. An abler pen than mine—that of Mr. Huntington—early familiar with him in all relations, of kindred powers and aims, associated with him officially and socially, and his successor in the presidency of the National Academy of Design, bears witness to these points in the *Memorial Address:*—

'Durand was endowed with certain traits which combined to form a great artist. He was early smitten with the love of nature ; his native patience was strengthened by the severity of his early struggles, and to these was added an indomitable perseverance. His love of nature was a passion, an enthusiasm always burning within him ; but it was like a steady fire, not a sudden blaze quickly sinking to ashes. His patience enabled him to guide this intense delight in beauty into paths of quiet, steady search for the result. It was touch after touch, line upon line, a gradual approach to victory. Added to this was his untiring perseverance, which no difficulties could overcome, no obstacles diminish, or even cold indifference discourage. Though full of nervous energy, alive to every beauty, keenly sensitive to criticism, and a severe critic on his own work, he was yet blessed with a certain serenity of spirit which checked and soothed the restless fever of the creative brain ; a fever often so violent in the painter or the poet as to cause a deep and sometimes fatal reaction and depression. Durand formed a habit of working on and on cheerily till the coveted prize was gained.

'He maintained that a landscape-painter in his early studies should not only make careful copies of nature in the fields, but be trained by drawing the human figure, both from the antique and from the living model. Accuracy of eye, with facility and exactness, can rarely, if ever, be acquired without such practice. Such a training quickly asserts itself in the modelling of forms in mountain, rock, and forest, in cloud structure, the lines of waves, &c. The forms of inanimate nature seldom demand absolute accuracy of drawing; but in accessory figures, buildings, and animals, it is essential. Durand, through his drilling as an engraver of figures, and especially of portraits, was habitually true and exact; yet he dwelt with great fondness on those qualities which depend on the processes and mysteries of the art, the rendering of subtle and infinitely varying effects of atmosphere, of fleeting clouds, mist, sunshine, twilight obscurity, and the thousand wondrous phenomena which form the peculiar glory of landscape.

'The whole fraternity of artists were proud of his achievements, reverenced his character, and looked up to him with affection. In the midst of the beautiful surroundings of his home, in a house standing on the spot where he was born, he tranquilly passed a serene old age, modestly wearing the laurels won by the faithful struggles of a noble and useful life; and patiently submitting himself to the will of God, calmly awaited the summons which, on the 17th day of September, 1886, at the venerable age of ninety years, called him to the eternal life beyond.'

It is only necessary to add that the Rev. Dr. Clover, his pupil and friend, officiated at the funeral ceremony, and that the interment took place in Greenwood Cemetery.

There are several portraits of my father. The first one is by Wm. Jewett, painted before 1825. After this comes a portrait painted by Colonel Trumbull in 1826, and, next, another painted by E. Metcalf about 1830. He painted his own portrait for the National Academy of Design about 1835. Mr. W. T. Walters commissioned C. L. Elliott to paint a portrait of him, now in his possession. In 1864 a copy was made by Mr. Elliott for Mr. S. P. Avery, who published an engraving of it by John Halpin. This copy, bought of Mr. Avery by Mr. John Taylor Johnston, is now in the Corcoran Gallery at Washington. Mr. Huntington painted a portrait of him for the Century Club, representing the artist seated on a knoll under trees, engaged on

E E

the picture of 'Franconia Notch.' Rowse made an excellent drawing in the possession of the writer. A bust by H. K. Brown, modelled in 1854, is in the possession of the National Academy of Design. There is a medallion by Kuntze, a cameo medallion by Saulini, made in Rome in 1840, and a medal bearing his head by Muller, issued by the Artists' Fund Society.

My task is finished. This work is an attempt to exhibit the life of an American artist dependent for the development of his talent on the natural taste for art in the community in which his lot was cast. Whatever his artistic merits may be, his rank in the profession will be assigned him by posterity. If I have succeeded in explaining his career by documents that furnish some idea of his sentiments, associations, and experiences, and have been able to arouse interest in the life of one who loved nature and portrayed its beauty as he found it to the best of his ability, my efforts have not been in vain.

APPENDIX.

I.

Extracts from 'Letters on Landscape Painting,' published in the ' Crayon,' 1855.

'DEAR SIR,

'I am compelled to return an unfavourable answer to your application for admission into my studio as a pupil. Among the many instances in which I have found it necessary to return a refusal, your case most interests me, on account of the earnest love of nature you manifest, and the strong desire you express to devote your whole time and energies to the study of Landscape Art. I hope the disappointment will not be regarded by you as discouraging, for I can readily imagine you may have over-estimated the advantage of such lessons as you desire at my hands, and I take occasion to submit for your consideration, by way of encouragement, some remarks resulting from my own experience under circumstances very similar to your own. With the same *love* of beautiful nature from my childhood, and the corresponding desire for *its* development through the knowledge and practice of Art, I was, by several years, older than yourself before I was able to devote even a small portion of my time to the favourite pursuit. I then thought as you now think, that if I could but obtain a few lessons by seeing an experienced artist work, or working myself under his eye and direct instructions, most happy should I be. That privilege, however, I never enjoyed; and subsequent years of toil and study have somewhat modified my estimate of the value of such privileges. Indeed, I am almost certain that instead of any real benefit resulting from it, the greater chance is, that in most instances it will prove pernicious.

'It is true that the pupil may thus save time in the acquisition of

certain technical knowledge, mechanical processes, most suitable colours,
&c.; at the same time he is, at least, in danger of losing his individuality,
and from the habit of seeing with the eyes and following in the track
of his master, becoming in the end what is most offensive in the mind
of every true artist, a mere imitator, a mannerist.

'You need not a period of pupilage in an artist's studio to learn
to paint; books and the casual intercourse with artists, accessible to
every earnest young student, will furnish you with all the essential mechanism of the art. I suppose that you possess the necessary knowledge
of drawing, and can readily express with the lead pencil the forms and
general character of real objects. Then let me earnestly recommend
to you one STUDIO which you may freely enter, and receive in liberal
measure the most sure and safe instruction ever meted to any pupil—
the STUDIO OF NATURE.

'Go first to Nature to learn to paint landscape, and when you shall
have learnt to imitate her, you may then study the pictures of great
artists with benefit. They will aid you in acquiring the knowledge
requisite to apply the skill you possess to the best advantage—to select,
combine, and set off the varied beauty of nature by means of what, in
artistic language, is called treatment, management, &c. I would urge
on every young student in landscape-painting, the importance of painting
direct from Nature as soon as he shall have acquired the first rudiments
of Art. If he is imbued with the true spirit and can appreciate and
enjoy the contemplation of her loveliness, he will find in the conscien-
tious study of her beauties all the leading principles of Art. Let him
scrupulously accept *whatever* she presents him, until he shall, in a degree,
have become intimate with her infinity, and then he may approach her
on more familiar terms, even venturing to choose and reject some portions
of her unbounded wealth. . . . .

'True Art teaches the use of embellishments which Nature herself
furnishes; it never creates them. . . . . If you should ask me to define
conventionalism, I should say that it is the substitution of an easily
expressed falsehood for a difficult truth. . . . .

'Form is the first subject to engage your attention. Take pencil and paper, not the palette and brushes, aud draw with scrupulous fidelity the outline or contour of the objects you select, and, so far as your judgment goes, choose the most beautiful or characteristic. If your subject be a tree, observe particularly wherein it differs from those of other species : in the first place, the termination of its foliage, best seen when relieved on the sky, whether pointed or rounded, drooping or springing upward ; next mark the character of its trunk and branches, the manner in which the latter shoot off from the parent stem, their direction, curves, and angles. Every kind of tree has its traits of individuality—some kinds assimilate, others differ widely ; with careful attention these peculiarities are easily learned, and so, in a greater or less degree, with all other objects. By this course you will obtain the knowledge of that natural variety of form so essential to protect you against frequent repetition and monotony. A moment's reflection will convince you of the vital importance of drawing, and the continual demand for its exercise in the practice of outline, before you begin to paint.

'I know you will regard this at first thought as an unnecessary restriction, and become impatient to use the brush, under the persuasion that you can with it make out your forms, and at the same time produce colour and light and shade. In this you deceive yourself, as many others have done, till the evil has become irremediable ; for slovenly and imperfect drawing finds but a miserable compensation in the evident efforts to disguise or atone for it, by the blandishments of colour and effect. . . . .

'Although there are certain principles constantly guiding the hand of the true artist, which can be defined, classified, and clearly understood, and, therefore, communicable—yet the history of Art from the beginning does not present a single instance where a thorough and scientific knowledge of these principles has of itself produced a truly great artist, for the simple reason that such knowledge never can create the feeling which, overruling all principles, gives the impress of true greatness. I caution you, therefore, against reliance on theoretical or technical directions which I or any one else may give in the course of your studies, further than as means which you are to employ subject to your own feeling. . . . .

'Waste not your time on *broad sketches* in colour ; such only can be useful to the mature artist, as suggestive rather than representative. You had better look at all objects more with reference to light and dark than colour ; but do not infer from this that I would depreciate the value of colour, for it is of inestimable value.   It is, however, a sort of humoursome sprite or good demon—often whimsical and difficult of control—at times exceedingly mischievous, spoiling many a good picture as if with mere malicious intent ; but when experience shall have acquainted you with its tricks and its virtues, you will understand better the worth of its service.

' " You had better learn to make shoes," said the venerable Colonel Trumbull, one day, to a stripling who was consulting him in reference to his choice of painting as a profession—" better learn to make shoes or dig potatoes than to become a painter in this country."   I felt that this was a harsh repulse to the young man, and most unexpected from such an authority.   I was not then a painter, but secretly hoping to become one.   I felt a strong sympathy for the victim, and thought he was unkindly treated ; but I can now imagine that there might have appeared to the mind of the veteran artist sufficient ground for such advice, and that it may have been an act of kindness rather than severity.   It is better to make shoes, or dig potatoes, or follow any other honest calling to secure a livelihood, than seek the pursuit of Art for the sake of gain. . . . . Through such motives the Art becomes debased, and a picture so painted, be its subject landscape or figure, may well be considered but an empty decoration.   But, fortunately for Art, such is not its true purpose ; it is only through the religious integrity of motive, by which all real artists have ever been actuated, that it still preserves its original purity, impressing the mind through the visible forms of material beauty with a deep sense of the invisible and immaterial, for which end all this world's beauty and significance, beyond the few requirements of our animal nature, seems to be expressly given. . . . .

' To appreciate Art, cultivation is necessary, but its power may be felt without that ; the feeling educates itself into the desired appreciation, and derives from it a corresponding degree of pleasure, according to the purity or depravity, the high or low character, of the Art that awakens it. . . . . .

'I have already advised you to aim at direct imitation, as far as possible, in your studies of foreground objects. You will be most successful in the more simple and solid materials, such as rocks and tree-trunks, and, after these, earth-banks and the coarser kinds of grass, with mingling roots and plants, the larger leaves of which can be expressed with even botanical truthfulness ; but when you attempt masses of foliage or running water, anything like an equal degree of imitation becomes impracticable.

'It should be your endeavour to attain as minute portraiture as possible of these objects, for although it may be impossible to produce an absolute imitation of them, the effort to do so will lead you to a knowledge of their subtlest truths and characteristics ; thus, knowing thoroughly that which you paint, you are able the more readily to give all the facts essential to their *representation*. This excessively minute painting is valuable, not so much for itself as for the knowledge and facility it leads to.

'There is a marked distinction between *imitation* and *representation*, and if this distinction be at first difficult to comprehend, it will become more and more apparent as you advance. Although painting is an imitative Art, its highest attainment is representative, that is, producing such resemblance as shall satisfy the mind that the entire meaning of the scene represented is given.

'Truth of colour and general harmony, whether of warmth or coolness, will satisfy every eye ; if the picture fails in these it is false somewhere, while if the artist devotes himself with overweening fondness to a preconceived notion of any particular *quality* of colour, without a primary regard to truth in its adaptation to his subject, he can scarcely fail to produce an incongruity, and thus fix the attention of the observer on the nice mixture of pigments rather than on the sentiment of his work. Nothing is more common among pretentious critics, as well as artists, than commendations of this and that picture for certain *fine qualities* of colour ; it is a favourite theme with the conventionalist, and when these peculiar qualities evince extraordinary skill, all other considerations are thrown aside, and the painter becomes distinguished for that alone. Thus many a young artist is sadly misled, seeking for something that he does not see or feel, and blindly falling into servile imitation of some prominent leader in the display of these much-lauded qualities. . . . .

‘All the best artists show that the greatest achievement, in the producing of fine colour, is the concealment of pigments and not the parade of them ; and we may say the same of execution. The less apparent the means and manner of the artist, the more directly his work appeals to the understanding and the feelings. I shall never forget the reply of Allston to some friends who were praising a very young student in Art for great cleverness, especially in the *freedom* of his execution. “Ah,” said he, “that is what we are trying all our lives to get rid of.” With that he opened a closet, and brought out a study of a head that he had painted from life, when a young man, at one sitting, and placed it beside a finished work on his easel, at which we had been looking. “There,” said he, “that is freely painted.” No other comment was required ; in the one, paint and the brush attracted attention, in the other neither was visible, nothing but the glow of light and colour which told its truth to Nature— and thus it is with the works of all the greatest colourists. Their skill lies in the concealment of the means by which the desired effect is attained ; consequently their productions defy the sagacity of the critical examiner to detect any specific mixture or compound by which their characteristic excellence has been attained. It is neither warmth nor coolness that elicits admiration, force nor delicacy, high key nor low key ; but always harmony and entire subordination of means. Now, we are not to suppose that this subordination has been especially aimed at by the artist, but that it is the consequence of the process by which higher aims have been reached.

‘Execution is simply the mode of applying paint to the canvas. It is praiseworthy when it gives assurance of correctness in drawing, and of the knowledge and feeling that have guided the hand. Too much importance is often attached to it, and the young artist is apt to regard it as one of the first objects of his pursuit, instead of the natural consequence of his practice. Your execution will be good in proportion to your knowledge and skill in drawing ; when it becomes conspicuous as a principal feature of the picture, it is presumptive evidence, at least, of deficiency in some higher qualities. So, your colouring will more likely be good, or even excellent, when it does not arrest the attention, and thus divert the eye and mind from the superior considerations of design, composition, and character. . . . .

‘ Servile imitation, so called, is difficult to understand. If its meaning is limited to that view of realism which accepts commonplace forms and appearances, without searching for the ideal of beauty, the objections are valid ; but if it comprehends the faithful representation of all that is most beautiful and best fitted for the purposes of Art, really existing and accessible, and ever waiting to be gathered up by earnest love and untiring labour, then is it an utter fallacy, born of indolence and conceit. With the faculty to perceive and select from the infinite beauty and significance of Nature, surely no artist can reasonably complain for lack of unbounded liberty. Imitation of Nature is indeed servile, and every way unworthy, when it discards the necessity of selection. . . . .

‘ I desire not to limit the universality of Art, or require that the artist shall sacrifice aught to patriotism ; but, untrammelled as he is, and free from academic or other restraints by virtue of his natal position, why should not the American landscape-painter boldly originate a high and independent style, based on his native resources ?— ever cherishing an abiding faith that the time is not far remote when his beloved Art will reflect the fine scenery of his “ own green forest land,” and secure for the artist as fair a coronal as ever graced a brow “ in that Old World beyond the deep.”

‘ Truly yours,

‘ A. B. Durand.’

F F

II.

Reply of Horatio Greenough to a criticism by George William Curtis on the picture, 'God's Judgment upon Gog,' published in the ' New York Tribune,' 1852.

'*To the Editors of the* HOME JOURNAL.

' GENTLEMEN,

'I find in the *Daily Tribune* of May 20th [1852], under the rubric of "Fine Arts," a criticism of Mr. Durand's picture of the destruction of Gog and his host, which seems to me to deserve a moment's attention. It commences as follows :—

' "Whatever Mr. Durand does is undeniably excellent. We had the pleasure, last year, of recording at some length our impression of his characteristics as a painter. His position is assured. A quiet, pastoral poet—a Thomson on canvas—always soothing, never inspiring—sure to please, equally sure not to surprise—a careful and loving student and imitator of the placid aspect of nature, and a genius that breathes pastoral peace over all his works—such was, in general, our feeling of Mr. Durand as an artist. It has been confirmed from year to year. There has been little marked advance, within our recollection, although certainly no retrocession. As with Bryant in poetry, it does not seem that the artist's experience deepens and widens with time. What they paint or sing to-day, they might have painted and sung twenty years ago. Without insinuating that either painter or poet suggests the remark, it is yet true that he who labours to preserve a reputation will be very apt to cease to deserve it. The stern claim made upon every artist, of whatever department, is to leave what he has done behind him, in his perpetual passage to greater achievements. It is a terrible law, but we are all held to it. And the history of illustrious men is the story of their unceasing advance."

' You will remark that the critic gives Messrs. Bryant and Durand each a sugar-plum and a box on the ear. They are bidden to be content with *respectability* and *excellence.* They are told that they can never surprise, and, lest the slap should fail to reach them, they are reminded shortly afterward that *greatness* always *surprises*. Disclaiming any intent to belittle these men, he asserts that " he who labours to preserve a reputation will seldom deserve it." Not satisfied with judging the work of Durand for what it is intrinsically, the critic lugs in Raphael and Kaulbach, and coolly measures the stature of the President of the School of Design. He cites before his anonymous authority two very able men, and thrusts upon their brows two small garlands of " Daphne's deathless plant," seeking the while to sting them to the quick by a poisoned thorn wreathed with the verdure of approbation. *Is this fair criticism?*

' It is a strain of remark seldom applied to the works of those that are passed away, yet, to my reason and feeling, is singularly uncourteous and offensive as towards contemporaries. If either of the gentlemen thus dealt with were a hero of the hour—mounted upon vogue, and riding roughshod over a blinded public, debasing the general taste by claptrap, or filling his pockets by the hurried abuse of certain popular elements of effect, I would understand such asperity, and perhaps excuse it. As it stands, it looks to me very like an outrage—coming from under cover, a mean outrage.

' An impartial public does not thus judge those whose study and labours are devoted to the best and purest enjoyments of society. An impartial public does not, in accepting the fruit of any man's genius, flout him by trumpeting some one else, and thus send him away with a flea in his ear.

' Charles Churchill undervalued the genius of Hogarth. He sought to stamp him as one who, in a world of beauty, saw only vice to lash and deformity to ridicule ; but this talk about Hogarth, thus presented in the garb of criticism and approbation, too, was only personal hate and spite in disguise. A contemporary of D. Teniers might easily have wounded his feelings by setting forth the greatness of the styles he never attempted, and lauding his ale-house scenes and groups of peasantry, but collective manhood would soon deal justly with such criticism. Collective manhood would see in such talk about the grand style, only a bullet ; in such praise behind it, the gun-cotton intended to send it home. In short, a grudge against old David, and no special love of painting. Collective manhood has silence for the failures of able men, and joy and reward for their success. It is often your individual who has been socially *froissé*, or perhaps overshadowed, who lets off a petard of this kind under the seat where the approved have been placed by opinion.

'With the long and clever discussion about the difference of the old and new dispensations I have nothing to do, but will remark in passing that the writer seems well fitted to handle such matters. He has the acumen and the rancour adapted to theological problems. There is one quotation, however, in the article singularly at war with its general spirit, and, to my sense, worth all the rest of it, "Little children, love one another!"

'Let us hope that the frame of mind in which this criticism of Durand was written is not habitual. If it be so, then doth the writer inhabit a little hell of his own, from which we wish him a speedy deliverance. We wish it truly; for we have remarked that only your originally sweet wine will sour to a vinegar of such acrid proof.

'Yours,

'An Artist.'

'*To the Editors of the* Home Journal.

'Gentlemen,

'I had occasion, a few weeks since, to complain of the spirit in which a correspondent of the *Tribune* had ventured to state not only what Mr. Durand is, but what he thought that painter lacks of "greatness." I wish now to say a few words about a "terrible law" to which "we are all held," to leave behind us our past works in a constant march towards perfection.

'I have known many terrible laws, but they were all human laws, and, in the long run, proved just as foolish as they were terrible. I have known several men of undoubted genius, and never found them groaning under a sense of oppression of the kind set forth in the *Tribune*. The man of genius is pre-eminently the servant of a God whose service is perfect freedom. This terror—this delirium tremens—of responsibility belongs, I believe, rather to what is called talent, especially when con-joined with a fierce desire to *parvenir*, as the French say—to succeed.

'Your man of genius goes about looking for responsibility ; and when he finds it, he takes it joyfully, often telling you, somewhat frankly, that he is the man for it, and forgetting, in the fervour of his volition, that modesty which the copy-books have conjoined inseparably with merit. He not only promises largely, magnificently, but he tells you that his performance is not to be despised—*Exegi monumentum ære perennius ! Regalique situ pyramidum altius.* That's the way he talks when he is communicative and in good humour with himself.

'I believe it is Ovid who shows his conviction of the immortality of the soul by loudly defying old "*tempus edax rerum*" to strike one leaf from his laurelled brow.

'Dante says that he writes from a harmony, that *suona dentro* inside of him. He accuses no terrible pressure from without, except political tyranny and want of bread. *L'altrui pane*—eating the crust of charity —that is his complaint. Shakespeare's "eye in a fine frenzy rolling," rolled from the fulness of the God within, not from fear of outward look or black mark in the *Tribune*.

'I am afraid that some of our critics, with their stern claims and terrible law, have swallowed more of the east wind than is good for the liver. They may do harm with this reign of terror. Boys of genius are sprouting in every direction, by all accounts. Why scare them in this way ?

'Look at Robert Burns ! When he brought forward his little speci-mens of the utterance of genius, the dominant intellect of Britain said, "It is naught!" So they set him to gauge whiskey ; yet, when he had gone his way, "straightway they rejoiced !" built him a huge monument, and bemoaned him. So far from making any stern claim upon this mind, now known as the very jewel of Scotland, the dunderheads never found out what he was good for until he was gone. Burns hankered and cankered—he confessed it—but it was not for fear of not getting utter-ance : it was, he says, "to see their cursed pride." They made stern claims of some kind or other, and he protested against them. There is little doubt that the man saw in the distance the big marble monument that was to shelter his image. He would gladly have exchanged some tithe of its future outlay and splendour, and have received therefor a cottage for his wife and bread for his bairns. What terror inspired his song? If I mistake not, he says, roundly, " I rhyme for fun."

' Though my hair is now fast whitening, I remember, as it were but yesterday, my wedding-day. The parson who officiated on that occasion was one of these " terrible law " people ; he made my Mary weep, and I gave him, internally, an Irish blessing. Now, I have never found, during a long life, any of the terrible business he talked about. We prefer each other now as we did then—at least that is my position ; and when I trace in our boys the joint resemblance, my heart expands with such proof of sympathy.

' Genius would seem to make immense efforts, almost unconsciously, and to keep a large reserve out of the fight altogether. Shakespeare went into the country and remained still. He has told us that he knew his name would have a life where life is most active, " even in the mouths of men." Lord Bacon, too, pointed out his future station in the world's opinion, adding, mournfully, that it must be withheld " until some time be passed away." This disposition on the part of mediocrity to harry and scourge and flout men of creative power, looks more like the result of a terrible law than anything else in the annals of genius. Still, it is too general not to be an ordinance of God. Like loves like, and it requires the collective heart of man to made a quorum to judge the broad, the deep, the genial soul. The man of vast power of mind is like the fortress full of armed hosts, with spears glittering over the turret, with pointed artillery and burning match. We set down to sketch it and glorify it more cordially when the portcullis chain is broken, the guns are spiked, and the ivy and the owl have possession of its towers.

' Yours truly,

' An Artist.'

III.

LIST OF ENGRAVINGS BY A. B. DURAND.

PORTRAITS.

Old Pat, *after a study from life by Waldo.*

John Trumbull, author of ' M'Fingall,' *after the portrait painted by Col. John Trumbull.*

James Otis.

Franklin, *after a medallion.*

Rev. James Milnor.

Rev. Alexander McLeod, D.D.

Rev. Henry Wilbur.

Rev. Samuel H. Cox, D.D.

Rev. J. B. Matthies.

Rev. Wm. Ross.

Rev. Hugh Blair, D.D.

Rev. Richard Reese.

Rev. Joshua Soule.

Rev. Elijah Woolsey.

Rev. Wm. Phœbus.

Rev. Elijah Hedding.

Rev. Laban Clark.

Rev. James B. Finley.

Rev. Wm. Patton.

Rev. J. M. Matthews.

Rev. Philip Milledoler.

Rev. J. B. Romeyn, D.D.

Rev. John Wesley (*copy*).

Rev. Gardner Spring.

Rev. Sylvester Larned.

Rev. John Summerfield.

Rev. John M. Mason, D.D., *after a portrait by Jarvis.*

Rev. Eliphalet Nott.

Rev. Edmund D. Griffin.

Rev. Nathaniel Bangs.

Rev. Dr. Dalcho.

Rev. Wm. Jay.

Rev. Wm. Sprague.

Benjamin West.

Ma-mencue.

Iturbide.

Oliver Wolcott.

Philip Hone.

Wm. Paulding, *after a drawing by the engraver.*

Cadwallader D. Colden.

John Hunter.

Noah Webster.

Adam Clarke, LL.D.

Michael Pekenino.

W. H. Crawford.

Judge Platt.

Anna Braithewaite.

PORTRAITS (*continued*).

Elias Boudinot.

Wm. Fuller, *after a drawing by C. C. Ingham.*

Major-General C. C. Pinckney.

John Quincy Adams, *after a portrait by Sully.*

Joseph O. Plessis.

Lindley Murray.

Wm. Floyd.

Wm. Pinkney.

Hugh Williamson, M.D.

Wm. Gibson, M.D.

Wm. Swaine, M.D.

Valentine Mott, M.D.

Philip S. Physick, M.D.

S. L. M. Mitchell, M.D.

Thomas Cooper, M.D.

David Hosack, M.D., *after the portrait by Sully.*

Lieut.-Col. Charles de Salaberry.

General Andrew Jackson, *full-length, after the picture by John Vanderlyn.*

John Trumbull, *after the portrait by Waldo and Jewett.*

Gilbert Stuart, *after a miniature by Sarah Goodrich.*

Isaac Shelby, *after the portrait by Jewett.*

Commodore Decatur, *after a copy by Herring of the portrait by Sully.*

Joel Barlow, *after the portrait by Robert Fulton.*

General Jacob Brown, *after the portrait by Jarvis.*

John Jay, *after the portrait by Stuart and Trumbull.*

Aaron Ogden, *after the portrait by the engraver.*

William Gaston, *after the portrait by G. Cooke.*

John Brooks, *after a copy by Herring of the original by Stuart.*

James Kent, LL.D., *after the portrait by Spencer.*

James Monroe, *after the portrait by John Vanderlyn.*

Alexander Hamilton.

David Crockett, *after the portrait by A. L. De Rose.*

John Marshall, LL.D., *after the portrait by Inman.*

Mr. Cowell.

Mr. Hilson.

Mr. Duff.

Mrs. Barnes.

Mr. Barnes.

Mrs. Hilson.

Mr. Macready.

Edwin Forrest.

George Jones.

James H. Hackett.

Stephen Van Rensselaer.

Rem Rapelje.

De Witt Clinton, *after a medallion.*

De Witt Clinton, *after the portrait by Inman.*

De Witt Clinton, *after the portrait by Ingham.*

PORTRAITS (*continued*).

Morgan Lewis.

Garrit Furman.

Robert C. Sands.

Catherine M. Sedgwick, *after the portrait by Ingham.*

George Washington, *after the portrait by Trumbull.*

George Washington, *after the portrait by Stuart.*

George Washington, *after a drawing by Miss Sparks from the bust by Houdon.*

Charles Carroll of Carrolton, *after a portrait by Harding.*

AMERICAN LANDSCAPE.

Weehawken, *after a view painted by W. J. Bennett.*

Catskill Mountains, *after a view painted by the engraver.*

Fort Putnam, *after a view painted by R. W. Weir.*

The Delaware Water-Gap, *after a view painted by the engraver.*

Falls of the Sawkill, *after a view painted by W. J. Bennett.*

Winnipiseogee Lake, *after a view painted by T. Cole.*

ILLUSTRATIONS FOR ANNUALS.

The Ghost of Darius, *after a picture by Inman.*

The Wife, *after a picture by Morse.*

The Dying Greek.

The Sisters, *after a picture by Morse.*

The Greek Boy, *after a picture by R. W. Weir.*

The Greek Lovers.

Gipsying Party, *after a picture by C. R. Leslie.*

William Tell.

The Power of Love.

The Dull Lecture, *after a picture by Stuart Newton.*

Anne Page, Slender, and Shallow, *after a picture by C. R. Leslie.*

The White Plume, *after a portrait by Ingham.*

The Bride of Lammermoor, *after a picture by Inman.*

Sancho Panza and the Duchess, *after a picture by C. R. Leslie.*

MISCELLANEOUS.

Head of St. Anthony.

Arrival of Hendrik Hudson.

The Declaration of Independence, *after the picture by John Trumbull.*

Musidora, *after a design by the engraver.*

Title-page for a volume commemorative of the opening of the Erie Canal, published by the City of New York.

Title-page for the *New York Mirror.*

Design for the Typographical Society.

Diploma for the New York Historical Society.

The Monument of Edmund Kean, St. Paul's Churchyard, New York.

Lady Lightfoot, racehorse.

Eclipse, racehorse.

Ball tickets and Business cards.

Vignettes, miniature portraits, and other designs for Bank-notes, estimated at one hundred in number.

Ariadne, *after the picture by John Vanderlyn.*

INDEX.

ERRATA.

Page 65, l. 4 from the bottom, *for* Fennimore *read* Fenimore.

Page 74, l. 2 from the top, *for* James B. Smillie *read* James D. Smillie.

London : Printed by Strangeways & Sons, Tower Street, Cambridge Circus, W.C.

ERRATA.

The following errors, mainly due to the conditions under which the proofs were read, must be noted by the reader :

Page 56, for *John Marshall, first chief-justice*, read John Marshall, chief-justice.

Page 56, for *Charles Carrol of Carrolton*, read Charles Carroll of Carrollton.

Page 57 and elsewhere, for *S. L. M. Mitchell*, read S. L. Mitchell.

Pages 59 and 60, for *Cary*, read Carey.

Page 62 and elsewhere, for *Charles Wilson Peale*, read Charles Willson Peale.

Page 67, Leslie was not " born on American soil " as stated, but in England, of American parents.

Page 80, for *Thomas Addis Emmett*, read Thomas Addis Emmet.

Page 102 and elsewhere, for *Smybert*, read Smibert.

Page 103, line 9, for *1776*, read 1774.

Page 103, line 16, for *1770*, read 1768.

Page 103, line 18, for *1774*, read 1770.

Page 103, line 21, for *1794*, read 1777.

Page 103, line 23, for *1872*, read 1811.

Page 104, line 17, for *more of an adventurer than the rest*, read more adventurous than the rest.

Page 192, Leutze, instead of being born in this country, was born in Nuremberg, Bavaria.

Page 201, line 2 from the bottom, for *historiographet*, read historiographer.

Page 224, for *Goodrich*, read Goodridge.

Page 224, for *Swaine*, read Swaim.   Omit *M.D.*

Page 232, index, for *Sir Benjamin West*, read Benjamin West.